"Diane Eshin Rizzetto does not really tel[] living a life that gives us hope; instead, she *shows* us how to find in ourselves the resources of a life of hope. And she does this by skillfully blending the teachings of the paramitas with actual practices and personal explorations that reveal the wisdom and power of these ancient teachings. By turning toward our own experience of the paramitas, we readers are offered a startling path through these dark times when hope is sorely needed."

—Roshi Pat Enkyo O'Hara, author of
Most Intimate: A Zen Approach to Life's Challenges

"Diane Rizzetto's *Deep Hope* is an inspirational guidebook grounded in the 'six perfections' teachings of Buddhism and leavened by her contemporary and practical style of Zen wisdom. The book reenvisions hope as a foundational approach to living 'based on the energy of life itself.' Each chapter is filled with pithy stories, teachings, student questions, and practices, which together offer readers a rich toolset to approach the deepest challenges of life—especially how to remain positive and engaged in today's confused and conflict-weary world. Society needs this book and will benefit in myriad ways from its timely wisdom."

—Lewis Richmond, author of
Aging as a Spiritual Practice

"*Deep Hope* is the very thing we need in days when despair is close at hand. With wisdom, eloquence, and ordinary words, Diane Eshin Rizzetto helps us see that enlightenment is an activity and that deep hope can be catalyzed by Buddhist practices of perfection, the six paramitas. These straightforward practices take us within and beyond ourselves to the shore of liberation. *Deep Hope* offers a clear map of the way."

—Hozan Alan Senauke, vice-abbot, Berkeley Zen Center,
and author of *The Bodhisattva's Embrace*

DEEP HOPE

Zen Guidance for Staying Steadfast When the World Seems Hopeless

Diane Eshin Rizzetto

SHAMBHALA
Boulder
2019

Shambhala Publications, Inc.
4720 Walnut Street
Boulder, Colorado 80301
www.shambhala.com

Much of the material in chapter 3, "Taking Skillful Action,"
is adapted from the author's previous book
Waking Up to What You Do (Boston: Shambhala, 2006).

9 8 7 6 5 4 3 2 1

First Edition
Printed in the United States of America

⊗ This edition is printed on acid-free paper that meets the
American National Standards Institute z39.48 Standard.
♻ This book is printed on 30% postconsumer recycled paper.
For more information please visit www.shambhala.com.

Shambhala Publications is distributed worldwide by
Penguin Random House, Inc., and its subsidiaries.

Designed by Greta D. Sibley

Library of Congress Cataloging-in-Publication Data
NAMES: Rizzetto, Diane Eshin, author.
TITLE: Deep hope: Zen guidance for staying steadfast
when the world seems hopeless / Diane Eshin Rizzetto.
DESCRIPTION: First Edition. | Boulder: Shambhala, 2019.
| Includes bibliographical references.
IDENTIFIERS: LCCN 2018026744 | ISBN 9781611804775
(pbk.: alk. paper)
SUBJECTS: LCSH: Paramitas (Buddhism)
CLASSIFICATION: LCC BQ4336 .R59 2019 | DDC 294.3/444—dc23
LC record available at https://lccn.loc.gov/2018026744

Contents

ACKNOWLEDGMENTS

APPRECIATION TO my teachers and students with whom I have been blessed to share this winding path of Zen practice. I also thank Barbara Gates, whose guidance helped me birth this book by guiding my words from thoughts to paper, and Diana Limbach Lempel, who offered clear and perceptive feedback on the early stages of the manuscript. And special thanks to Dave O'Neal, whose support has been a source of great encouragement through the years. Finally, my deep appreciation to my children, grandchildren, great grandchildren, and to my husband, Jay, for his love and support.

INTRODUCTION

EVERY DAY we receive news of cruelty and pain around the world. It's not easy to escape the knowledge of the suffering people are inflicting on other people, whether on our own block, in our own town, or across the world. The reality that we live in a world filled with danger and uncertainty seems to greet many of us when we wake each day. And the abundance of instant news and social media makes certain that we are immediately informed of the latest catastrophes—bombings, killings, natural disasters, abusive and unstable governments, and on and on. Anger, divisiveness, cruelty, fear, and hopelessness seem to be at the forefront of human affairs around the world.

And yet, sitting with my cup of tea each morning as I read the newspaper, I am struck by the contradictory behavior among people. On the one hand, there is much evidence of violence and division, and, on the other hand, a disaster such as an earthquake, flood, or terrorist attack can kick us into an immediate response to help others. In a split second, all that seems to separate us—skin color, religion, nationality—falls away, and we give of ourselves completely as our awareness turns toward the present moment and what needs to be done.

There is plenty of evidence that we are capable of turning our efforts to meet the reality of what is, of taking compassionate action because it is the right thing to do.

Yet, as we go about our daily lives, we can easily lose touch with this fundamental human capacity to bridge our perceived separations and connect with others, and thus we isolate ourselves, planting seeds of suffering for ourselves and others. And it seems the more terror and pain we experience, the stronger our fear and our desire to protect ourselves and our loved ones become. So, we may find that we become more selective about what and who we will let into our awareness. We may tend to hold back, hold in, and enclose ourselves in a tight circle of protection in the mistaken assumption that such a circumstance and state of mind make us safe. Sadly, we often don't even know we're closing ourselves off from the richness of all that truly supports and sustains us. And because we do so, we open the path to fear, anger, despair, and hopelessness.

This book offers a different path, a different way to meet and engage in the reality of the world in which we live. It offers a path to reveal our deepest human capacity to give and receive, to patiently bear witness to whatever is arising in the moment, to take skillful action based on clarity and wisdom, to persevere with fortitude, and to rest in the silent stillness of each breath. In this way, it offers us not a path *to* deep hope, but a way to engage *through* deep hope.

Hope Is a Journey, Not a Destination

But what is hope itself? The most common assumption about hope is that it is a kind of optimism or belief that particular events and conditions will unfold in a way that results in a particular outcome. We may purposely cultivate a goal-oriented attitude, take action, and put forward determination and effort toward a specific end. Studies in medicine and psychology have shown that this type of hope may have some very positive effects on healing and recovery. Many of the world religions speak of having hope or not losing hope by holding firm to faith in the tradition, and many people find strength to carry on in this deep-seated faith and hope. Within the school of Zen Buddhism, however, hope is not encouraged because to focus on a particular future outcome turns us from fully realizing the present moment and thus leads to further suffering. My teacher, Charlotte Joko Beck, often advised her students to "give up hope," for it only diminishes present reality.

Over the years of my Zen practice, I've come to understand "hope" a little differently. Hope is multifaceted. There is the kind of hope that looks toward a specific outcome, such as hoping that one more treatment might cure a life-threatening disease, or that a second, third, or fourth chance might be the one that turns our addicted loved one in a healthy direction. There is also the kind of hope that ties activity to a goal; for example, if we work or study hard, we might one day be able to support our family better and give our kids the opportunities we didn't have. Refugees fleeing war, poverty, or starvation leave their homelands in hope of finding better conditions. Volunteers around the world offer their services in hope of alleviating suffering and helping others. In a conversation with my teacher, Joko, soon after she gave a lecture on "having no hope," I shared some serious concerns about the future of a loved one. I said to her, "I'm trying hard not to have hope." Without skipping a beat, she responded: "Why not? I certainly would have hope if it were my loved one!" In the classic

Zen way, she counseled me not to be attached to anything—not even to no hope! Hope, yes, but don't be attached to the outcome. Know the difference between what she called "vain hope," which is a closed system between us and a desired future outcome, and what can be called "deep hope," which makes no guarantees for any particular outcome. The former fails to appreciate the complexity of conditions that will arise with whatever comes to be, whereas the latter understands that, in the midst of impermanence and interdependence, we can only do our best.

Deep hope springs from the energy of life itself. Because it is embedded in the journey, not the destination, it sustains us no matter the outcome of a particular course of events. Deep hope is what comes forth when we open our hearts and minds to what we can offer and what we receive. It arises in stepping forward in skillful action with fortitude and courage that is grounded in patience and clarity. It asks us to turn our hearts toward the good that is possible, whatever the good may be. Deep hope is more than simple optimism or wishful thinking for a specific outcome. In fact, like all of Zen practice, deep hope asks us to dwell in the unknown—that open, spacious realm of possibility. Yes, we face things as they are, but deep hope draws no conclusions about the future, for the future is yet to be and is determined by many conditions—including, but not limited to, our actions right here and right now. So, although we see things as they are, we also aspire toward what they could be.

It was in deep hope that Martin Luther King, Jr. encouraged us to keep raising our voices in solidarity and marching "step by step"; the same hope that expressed, "I have a dream." Hope understood in this way goes beyond the probable to the possible. Because the future is wide open, anything is possible.

Václav Havel describes what I'm calling deep hope as a "state of the mind, not a state of the world. . . . It is an orientation of the heart; it transcends the world that is immediately experienced, and is anchored somewhere beyond its horizons. . . . [It is] the ability to work for something because it is good, not just because it stands a chance to succeed. . . . It keeps us above water and urges us to good works."[1]

Deep hope encourages us to carry on in spite of what the X-rays or blood tests show, the path our kids are taking, or yet another bout of anxiety and depression. It arises when we purposely engage in living in such a way as to nurture and sustain our deepest capacity to continue on, knowing that, in spite of what appears on the surface, there exists a fundamental love and connection between all things. We just need to make the effort to allow it to come forth and reveal itself to us. This is what this book offers: a path of hope that is revealed and sustained by the deepest qualities within all of us. These virtues may not always be obvious, but they are always there, waiting as portals through which to enter our daily living. The Buddhist teaching of the paramitas offers us this portal.

Hope arises with and is integral to the Paramita of Giving and Receiving—offering a smile and a nod to connect with a perfect stranger or pausing for a moment of gratitude when quenching our thirst with a refreshing glass of clean water. It arises in the Paramita of Taking Skillful Action as we aspire to engage in activity, carefully considering how to support rather than harm all beings. And when we aren't sure how or if our actions will have any desired effect, hope arises as in the Paramita of Practicing Patience, as we meet conditions as they are in each moment—taking one step at a time, focusing on the steps and not the destination. Deep hope also emerges through the Paramita of Engaging Effort, as we wisely use our energy and resources toward a steady-as-you-go engagement, savoring the journey. And hope appears in the deep stillness of the Paramita of Meditating, as well as in the Paramita of Seeing Clearly—the understanding that all of life is continually unfolding and interconnected. Through the cultivation of this wisdom, we can develop the hope that springs from knowing that everything is in a constant state of change, and because of this fundamental truth, all things are possible.

DEEP HOPE

What Are the Paramitas?

THE WORD *paramita* is traditionally translated as "perfection," which carries the meaning of "going beyond" or "transcending." A common metaphor is the crossing of a river, such that to practice the paramitas is to cross over from the shore of what my teacher called "the cocoon of self-absorption" to another shore, where we realize that our own well-being and the well-being of others, all beings, and even the planet are interconnected in a vast web of love, joy, pain, and sorrow. I think of the paramitas as fundamental functions of human life that enable us to make wise and compassionate responses in a world filled with suffering.

The Buddha often used the parable of a raft to describe the journey of those who endeavor to help others, whatever their circumstances. The parable contains four elements: the shore we are standing on, the distant shore, the expanse of water in between, and the raft. The shore we stand on includes fear and uncertainty, sickness, death, and all we do that causes pain and suffering to ourselves and others. What seems, at the outset, the distant horizon is the shore that includes a deep capacity to bear the suffering and take action that arises out of compassion and love for our fellow beings. There reside our deepest virtues as humans and freedom from suffering.

Those who undertake to cross between the two shores quickly learn that the river is not static in its width or flow. Sometimes it's a small trickle, like when we find our steps slowing down and pausing to take a few moments to sincerely engage with a street person: "How are you doing today?" Other times the distance between the two shores seems like a vast expanse, as when we witness actions of hate and killing or when our own words of hate echo in our ears. Whatever the distance, the Buddha reminds us that there is a raft that can ferry us across. The raft is his teachings, and the teachings are found embedded in our life as it is. From the vast fundamental wholeness of everything, we are each endowed with the capacity to meet life as it is. It is by living within and through the intention of engaging fully in the world—using caring, courageous, and wise action to help all beings—that we find the materials from which to construct our raft. And the shape and appearance of each of our rafts will grow out of what we face in our unique lives from day to day, moment to moment, breath to breath. Zen stories remind us to look no further than our nose. Nothing special, just using what is at hand and putting it to good use. The paramitas are always within our reach. We just need to engage them: giving and receiving, taking skillful action, letting conditions unfold naturally, using wise effort, resting in the open ground of meditation, and allowing clear seeing to guide us. The practice of the paramitas ferries us to our deepest capacity to love and do good. Though this capacity is always at hand, often we just don't see it. The practice of the paramitas offers us a chance to see ourselves and the world anew, again and again.

When I was a young child, I was troubled and confused after hearing the minister in church speak of heaven and hell. Pondering his words while watching my mother washing dishes at the kitchen sink, I asked her, "Where's hell? Where's heaven?" She answered, "When people do their best in the world, there's heaven; when they do their worst in this world, there's hell." I remember somehow being both relieved and hopeful that, not only was hell not a pit of fire waiting to consume me when I broke the rules, but also that I had some say in creating heaven, simply by doing my best. I now understand that my mother's comment placed the making of my world just where it needed to be—with me, wherever I find myself.

The Journey

The paramitas are most often expressed as nouns—states of mind and body. However, another way to approach them is as verbs—as continual evolving processes. This is a place where I think the metaphor of two shores can be misleading. In my view, "perfection" is not a state of "other shore" that we can literally attain and sustain. Rather, it's an ongoing process of perfecting. What the pages of this book present is not the destination but the journey, which is our life itself. Whether riding the waves, resting in the doldrums, or navigating a sudden tempest, if we paddle the raft in whatever way we can—with a paddle, hands, or even feet!—therein is hope. Therefore, the paramitas are both states and processes. It is the latter that I emphasize throughout this book, and this is why I give the paramitas in verb form: Giving and Receiving, Taking Skillful Action, Practicing Patience, Engaging Effort, Meditating, Seeing Clearly.

What Connects Us

We are all so skilled at discerning how we're different, but we don't know enough yet about how we're all the same. The paramitas also offer a path to discovering what you and I and everyone else share as human beings—not our beliefs or values, but rather *who* and *what* we are at the core of our collective being. We don't need to create these human virtues, for they're already an essential part of our being and are simply veiled. The good news is that they can be brought forth and expressed in the most ordinary interactions of living. We only need to explore what blocks or clouds them and intentionally bring them into our lives. We can lift the veil and allow what is most natural in us to come forth. This is our practice: to nudge them, cultivate them, and encourage them to come forth.

The paramitas help us turn our deepest aspirations into action. They guide, coax, and support us toward living what we want to become—as individuals, as nations, as beings on the earth. They remind us that we have a choice—to support life or to destroy it. They bring forth the bone and marrow of living through and being sustained by our deepest humanity.

The Process

> The problem with the world is that we draw the
> circle of our family too small.
> —Mother Teresa

Mother Teresa's words cut to the chase: we can name lots of problems in the world, but what it all comes down to is that our view of life is severely limited by the confines of what we perceive as a safety zone. Some of us think that zone extends no further than family and friends. Some of us allow in our neighbors or other kinds of community members. Some of us feel at home with others who practice the same religion or others of our region or country. But how many of us are able to draw our family circle as wide as the hemisphere, the planet, or the universe?

In addition to relationship and space, there is also the dimension of time. We are comfortable and feel safe when we think we know what the future holds, when we are certain we have some control over events. And yet, as the great teachings remind us, it is exactly this clinging to our personal view of what is real and true, what is good or bad, that causes us to suffer. Clinging causes suffering because it closes us off from the potential of not knowing—the potential of life itself. In Zen teaching, we call this "don't-know mind." It is the mind that steps out of the limited self-centered view of life into an all-expansive view of life's full potential. It doesn't mean don't act; it means act wisely. It is also true that our sense of the circle changes over time. If conditions are favorable, then there's a good possibility that we may naturally widen our circle. But when we sense that our own family, friends, or community is threatened, then we tend to contract our circle again.

This is our world today. Whether we explicitly acknowledge this truth or try to keep it at a distance—through our
busyness, blindness, or however we do it—there's no escape
because what happens to the individual down the street or
across the world affects each and every one of us. And how
each of us responds affects everyone else. So, more than ever, it's
imperative that as individuals we do what we can to cultivate
our deepest human inclinations. Even though our natural
propensities to be generous, open, and wise may at times come
forth spontaneously, they are so easily reburied. So, we have
to cultivate and sometimes coax them into the forefront of our
life. When just one person engages life with sincere giving and
receiving (the terms I am using to designate the first paramita,
commonly translated as "generosity"), it has an effect on
others. It has an effect whenever someone engages in actions
that support others rather than only fulfilling their personal
desires. Every time a person bears witness to the unfolding
of conditions and events with patient equanimity, puts forth
energy and action based on well-meaning intentions, or turns
toward silence and stillness to see clearly what is, it ripples out
into the world.

To study the paramitas is a process of studying the self.
It is also the process of living hope. They go hand in hand.
This book approaches the paramitas not as destinations (as
in "reaching the other shore") or as accomplishments (as in
achieving "perfection"), but rather as a way for us to engage
in a process that I like to think of as "picking and pecking."
When a chick is ready to come into the world, it begins poking
at one spot from the inside of the egg. At the same time, the
mother hen begins pecking the spot from the outside. Together,
they break open the shell, and the baby chick emerges into
the world. In the same way, by purposely engaging in the

six paramitas, we poke at the potential of what is ready to emerge—the full capacity of living. We begin with the intention, but then the work comes. This is where we must put effort or energy into the long stretch, for it takes courage, patience, and fortitude to bring our deepest potential to do good into the forefront of our life in the midst of uncertainty.

There's no timetable, but when we take up the way of Giving and Receiving (Dana), Taking Skillful Action (Shila), Practicing Patience (Kshanti), Engaging Effort (Virya), Meditating (Dhyana), and Seeing Clearly (Prajna), we support not just ourselves and those close to us but also the world. This is what makes the practice of the paramitas the practice of the *bodhisattva*—the person who takes up the vow, over and over, to do what she can to help all beings. Perfection is a process, never a destination. We don't have to become something else or get something else—we just have to stand in the life we are living and appreciate all of life to its fullest. It doesn't work to wait for someone else to fix us or the world, to make conditions more conducive to caring, generosity, and peace. Each of us creates the world through our every thought and action, so the responsibility lies with us. This is what we'll be doing together through the pages of this book. Each of us will have our own journey as we unpack our personal propensity toward or away from each paramita. Although I describe the work in a linear fashion, in the sense of moving through the paramitas one by one, in truth practicing with the paramitas is both linear and circular.

Engaging with the paramitas begins with intention—to purposely take action that engages the mind of, for example, giving. We may decide to exchange a few words with the street person we pass each day on our way to work. We may purposefully bring up the mind of Practicing Patience by deciding to listen completely to a coworker whom we have trouble listening to.

After doing this practice for some time, we will find that we begin running into resistance. This is the meaty and most powerful part of paramita practice. The path gets muddier as we trudge around our personal circle, noticing how very small it tends to be. We feel the edginess and frustration of listening to our coworker speak. We experience the urgency to bypass the person on the street.

As a guide to this process, I have found particularly useful the Three Tenets of the Zen Peacemakers:[1] not knowing, bearing witness, and skillful action. When we run into our own resistance, rather than judging it or trying to manipulate our thinking, we approach it with openness and curiosity. This allows us to drop all that we think we know about ourselves and the other person or the situation and make space for the discovery of more of what is. This, however, is not usually very comfortable. To let go of all we *think* we know can bring up strong feelings such as vulnerability, anxiety, and anger. But by bearing witness to our own experience and to that of others, we allow the circle to widen, and when it does, a deeper intelligence guides us into skillful action. We study the self and, by doing so, include others. Then, at some point— and I stress, perhaps just for one moment—we find that we are effortlessly living and offering ourselves without restraint. There is no giver and no receiver.

The Balanced Wheel

Another way I like to think of the paramitas is as spokes on a bicycle wheel. The Buddha likens human suffering to a wheel out of kilter. When a wheel is not balanced, then the ride in the cart is bumpy and even dangerous. So, as a good bicyclist knows, all the spokes of the wheel must be carefully balanced so that, together, they allow the rim of the wheel to flow smoothly over the ground. We can think of each of the paramitas as spokes on a wheel that reinforce each other to support us as we travel our life. When Giving and Receiving, Taking Skillful Action, Practicing Patience, Engaging Effort, Meditating, and Seeing Clearly are balanced, we can meet whatever kind of road we find ourselves on with balance and stability. However, life doesn't always give us smooth ground. In fact, the nature of human life is that the wheel will continually drop out of kilter—we lose a job, a partner leaves, illness and loss strike us or our loved ones. And what's more, we worry over the state of the planet, perhaps the most grievous of all the serious challenges we face together. It's not only easy, but likely, that we'll get out of kilter, so we need help. We need the paramitas to remind us that, as we travel through life, that which carries us, our wheels, will sometimes be in balance and sometimes not—and when they are not, we suffer. When the rubber hits the road, as the events of life come up to meet us, how we meet the road we find ourselves on depends on the balanced spokes of the wheel.

As we explore each of the six paramitas, it will also become evident that, together, they form an interlocking circular chain. Every paramita to some extent includes all the others. I have chosen to present them in the traditional order beginning with Giving and Receiving and concluding with Seeing Clearly, because there is a certain logic to a discussion that way. It would be misleading, however, to suggest that each particular paramita stands on its own or can be mastered before moving on to the next one. Just as the bicycle wheel can't move on one spoke, neither can any one paramita be practiced without all the others.

What is it, then, that starts the whole practice? What comes before Giving and Receiving? I would like to suggest that the very fact that you are holding this book in your hands at this moment is a functioning of Seeing Clearly, or wisdom, for it reflects the thought that gives rise to the aspiration to widen the circle. This aspiration is also referred to as *bodhicitta*—literally, "the thought of wisdom." Sometimes it is also described as a "passion" for awakening—not just a thought or an ideal to aspire to, but a fire to understand what we are, what life is, what it all means. I have sometimes heard people ask, "What's this thing we call 'life?'" (Certainly, this is my own question, one that has driven me since I was very young.) "Is there more than this?" "Is this all there is?" When I hear such questions, I'm also hearing an understanding that life is more than we may think it is—an understanding that is taking the form of questioning. It's doubt of a kind that, in Zen practice, we come to understand as our ally.

The Buddha's own bodhicitta arose when, as a young man, he ventured outside the confines of the walls of his father's palace. Having theretofore known nothing of the pain and suffering in life, he was confronted for the first time with sickness, old age, and death in the world, and a great question arose in him: "Is there a way for all people to be free of this suffering?" Each of us, in our own way, may reach a point in our life when we ask the same question and are inspired to lean into the edges of our own walls. This is not just some philosophical understanding but a genuine, complete shift of perspective concerning our place in and interaction with the world. Our intention is to benefit others, but the work begins with ourselves. We see ourselves in others and others in ourselves, and from there we begin our work.

Life as It Is: Our Only Teacher

At the Bay Zen Center in Oakland where I teach, we frequently recite this verse:

> *Life as it is, the only teacher;*
> *Being just this moment, compassion's way.*

How do we begin to meet what life sends our way, taking it as our teacher?

As I sit with my morning tea in my sunny, comfortable kitchen, reading stories in my newspaper, I am often moved to reflect on people's incredible capacities. The mother clutching her babies in a boat filled with refugees, crashing over treacherous waves in the middle of the sea in the pursuit of safety. A family sending its children overland with strangers in the hope they'll make it to the other side of a border where there's safety and opportunity for a sustainable life. These examples are the stories of great feats by ordinary people who are driven to draw on their fullest capacities to live and survive. Their situations leave them little option. For most of us, and certainly for those reading this book, our circumstances may not be so overtly destitute. But we don't choose our teachers. We are given whatever life we have, and it's up to us as to how fully we engage with it. Teachers come to us in all types of circumstances, and if we're ready to question and learn, the most ordinary events of our life can be transforming. In fact, the longer we practice, the more we find our teachers hidden in the cracks and crannies of our ordinary life.

Painting a Closet

My front hall closet desperately needed painting. As a child, I often accompanied my dad when he worked as a housepainter. He carefully tutored me on how to hold a paintbrush correctly, how to apply the paint smoothly, and how to clean up properly. Over the years, painting projects became one way I could reconnect with my dad. So, as I've always done in the past, I went out to our storage shed and found some paint, gathered the brushes, and set out to get started. But life had another agenda for me. Soon after I did the prep washing of the walls, my body reminded me that it no longer easily does that type of physical activity. I didn't want to listen to the aching back and impending headache, so I pushed a bit further. And my body pushed back. By the next morning, it was clear that if I were to carry out the teaching commitments I had planned, then I could not have it all. I could not paint the closet and fly to Portland, Oregon, for a teacher's conference or meet with my students at the Zen center. My aging body was forcing me to face choices that I didn't want to make. It was forcing me to face what was right in front of me. It strikes me how difficult it was for me, even after many years of Zen practice, to let go of what would seem like a not-so-significant activity, painting a closet. Who ever heard of a thirty-five-year veteran of Zen practice finding tears falling because she can't paint a closet!

But this is the stuff of living. What moves us deeply doesn't always make a lot of sense. And this is the stuff of practicing with the paramitas. When we find ourselves in situations like this, we have a choice: we can rail against what's happening, or we can turn and listen to its story, allowing it to become our teacher. As I paused for a moment, a clear, albeit smaller voice from within came forward: "Stop. Look. Listen." Over my years of Zen practice, I've come to welcome this voice more and more, for I have found that it always leads me into what is present and true in this very moment. It silences the "shoulds and coulds" and reminds me to "enter here"—this is your life rising up to greet you in this moment. Stop for just a moment. Look and listen to yourself and to what's presenting itself to you. This is your teacher. This is what's true. This is your life. As I put down the paintbrushes and engaged, I listened to what I like to call Practicing Patience—the voice of knowing deep inside that encourages us to open awareness and curiosity of what is. I heard the voice of Giving and Receiving encouraging me to let go and give over, and to receive. I began to consider the wise use of energy and intention—the voice of Engaging Effort.

There is a Zen koan that invites us to "save a ghost." This koan asks us first to invite out of the closet our deepest fears and to face them. What I realized was that I was facing the fear of losing a treasured connection with my dad and that in some deluded way, I believed by pushing a bit harder, hanging on to that paintbrush, ignoring the reality of my limitations, I could hang on to my dad's memory. Once this connection was clear, I was able to surrender to my husband the task of painting my closet.

Bringing the paramitas into our daily living will inevitably bring us face to face with much that we've stuffed into our own versions of the closet. Vulnerability is what wakes us at four in the morning. It's what causes our hearts to race and panic to rise in our throats. It's where our skin wears thin, where our armor and our self-contained walls cannot withstand the truth of what's happening. And because of this, it is the exact place we can recognize our interdependence with all things. This is how we become free, and it is where deep hope is to be found.

As I sit at my computer, writing these words, my husband paints the closet. As I apply Practicing Patience and Giving and Receiving, a ripening has taken place. Yes, it was so very hard to let go and give over, to open my hand and release my hold on the paintbrush, but in doing so, my husband was given the opportunity to receive and give back. Handing over the paintbrush to him carried more than just a way to get the job done, for this handing of the paintbrush was a letting go of many things. For with it, my husband connected to my dad in his own way. Hopefully, by giving an ear to receive my story, you, the reader, may find some connection to these words and will carry their flavor into your own life. The web expands to others. A ripening is taking place. This is what the practice of the paramitas offers us.

Beyond the Closet

And, beyond my closet, beyond my house, beyond the continent in which I live, an elderly couple in a tiny village of northern Greece shares whatever food they have, whatever their small cottage offers, with refugees seeking asylum inside the Macedonia border. When reporters ask them, "How long will you do this?" they simply answer, "As long as we can. We have no choice. There are people suffering and they need help." At the very same time, terrorists plan and carry out horrendous acts of cruelty on innocent people. This is the complex nature of being human. We are capable of great acts of kindness and horrendous acts of cruelty. We can extend our hand in a generous offering that transcends real and perceived boundaries, or we can retreat behind those same boundaries and close off and isolate, creating "them and us."

As we explore the paramitas throughout this book, we will approach them as tools or skillful means that help us tap into our deepest human capacity to love and care for one another by inquiring, and sometimes coaxing, into the light what shadows that capacity. At the same time, we will look toward the paramitas as beacons directing us toward all that we are at the core. That this is a process cannot be overstated. Insights may occur in moments or in years. The discussions and exercises in the following pages are offered in the spirit of guided exploration for each person to engage in their own discovery and in their own ripening. The paramitas remind us that we have a choice. As the ancient teachings have taught us:

> *The thought manifests as words;*
> *The word manifests as deeds;*
> *The deed develops into habit;*
> *And the habit into character.*
> —The Buddha, *The Dhammapada*

2

Giving and Receiving
Dana Paramita

Something we were withholding made us weak
Until we found out that it was ourselves
We were withholding from our land of living . . .
—Robert Frost, "The Gift Outright"

In the Islamic tradition, it's called *zakat*. In the Jewish tradition, it's called *tzedakah*. In Christianity, it's called *charity*. And within Hinduism and Buddhism, it's called *dana*. No matter what it is named, the open abundance of the life force is forever giving forth. However, we don't always recognize this, and as a result, we unwittingly seek our sustenance by trying to acquire more from others and give less of ourselves. We contract rather than expand the circle of our hearts and minds.

The Circle of Giving and Receiving

As is true for all the paramitas, the Paramita of Giving and Receiving is a cyclical transformation. We begin by making an explicit, conscious effort to enact generosity. We make an outward gesture of our deepest capacity toward letting go into openness. At the same time, we look toward receiving, making an effort, perhaps a gesture, that affirms that we receive as well as give. Finally, forming full circle, our receiving turns to thanks as we give forth gratitude.

Imagine that you arrive for a dinner invitation and are placed at a long table laden with a bountiful feast—dishes of luscious food just waiting for everyone to partake. The host invites everyone to begin eating, but when you lift your eating utensil, you find it's ten feet long—so long that it's impossible for you to turn the utensil to reach your mouth. You try all kinds of ways to maneuver the utensil to feed yourself, but to no avail. As you grow more hungry and frustrated, what could have been a marvelous feast turns into a hellish nightmare. Then, quite naturally, the person opposite you lifts her long fork and offers the food to you from across the table. You open your mouth to receive her offering. Your tongue savors the rich abundance of the food. You pick up your fork and do the same for her. Before too long, everyone at the table is enjoying the marvelous feast as they give and receive the offering before them.

This story can be told from any cultural vantage point. The utensils can be ten-foot-long chopsticks, five-foot fingers, or the Brobdingnagian forks I described above. The feast could be fried rice, stuffed grape leaves, kababs, raw fish, or roast turkey. The guests could be sitting on chairs around a table or on the floor in a circle. No matter the cultural heritage, the fundamental human capacity to nourish and care for each other by the simple acts of giving and receiving remains the same. We need only reach out of the circle of *us* and *them*, to include *me* and *you*. This is the teaching of this story. It points to what the Paramita of Giving and Receiving offers us—the possibility to recognize and partake in the richness of all that we can offer to others and the opportunity to be nourished and sustained by offerings we never even knew existed. Our perspective shifts as the circle widens into possibility. This is the fuel that ignites hope.

Widening the Circle

The practice of giving and receiving first wakens us to the realization that we have enclosed ourselves in a small circle—a circle that shrinks the world into a space in which we feel safe. It encourages us to name that "something we are withholding." Then it coaxes us into leaning into the edges of our comfort zone to finally open to the abundance of life itself. The mistake of our thinking—that which keeps us enclosed in our circle, is not a lack of what is offered, but a blindness to seeing all that we offered.

Frost's poem suggests that that which we withhold makes us weak until we find that what we withhold is ourselves. And when we withhold ourselves, we withhold from life and living. The practice of the first paramita asks us to first consider the *something* we are withholding and to realize the greatest gift we can give is *ourselves*.

Wrapping Empty Boxes

What you give away, you keep; what you keep
you lose.
—A Lakota saying

It was Christmas, and at that particular time in my life I was sixteen years old, had a small baby, and was pregnant with my second child. My first marriage was a struggle in all sorts of ways. My husband was sick, we often didn't have enough money, and, of course, we were very young. That year, we had no money for food or rent, let alone to buy Christmas presents. But the lack of food and the rent money wasn't what troubled me most. What upset me was the thought that my baby's first Christmas didn't match the image of what I thought Christmas should be—lots of pretty, glitzy gifts for her to unwrap on Christmas morning to paint the perfect picture.

I felt miserable. If only there were a few presents under the tree, then I could feel better. So, I gathered up bits and pieces of ribbon and paper and a lot of empty boxes—soap boxes, anything I could find—and I wrapped these empty boxes up and placed them under a little tree. And those pretty little packages kept my illusion sweetly contained and safe, at least until Christmas morning when, of course, there was nothing to open but glitzy wrapped empty boxes.

Over the years, this experience has transformed into my koan, a riddle that pushes me to stretch the boundaries of my circle. What is it exactly that I was wrapping up? There are empty boxes that have nothing in them, and there are empty boxes that are filled to capacity. Empty? Full? Which is it? Each year, it seems I learn something new. Today, living conditions are different for me, but the story serves as a constant reminder when I turn away from the true conditions presenting themselves as my life. Looking under the Christmas tree, I saw a box as empty, something missing in my life; but what is this thing I call empty? What was inside was the sadness, the longing, the shame. But also, the box was full of the generosity of a young mother doing the best she could for her baby. Yes, creating a pretty picture, but in doing so, making an effort to give joy, love, and happiness. The box was hardly empty; it was bursting at the seams. Sometimes we think that what we have to offer is not enough—a box that is empty, or only partially filled. A deeper understanding of the Paramita of Giving and Receiving reminds us that intention is already a kind of fullness. The gift we truly have to offer is, in fact, *ourselves*. But do we really believe it's enough? Is our life enough?

It is a rare gift to simply meet with openness and clarity what life brings our way, to meet ourselves and others, to give and receive as we are at any given moment. We have the very mistaken belief that it's simply not enough. So, we wrap ourselves up in our images, which were themselves created by deep beliefs about "not enough" or "too much." We meet the conditions of our work, our relationships, our politics, and our finances not as they are but wrapped up with glitzy ideas about the way they *should be*. We try to make lots of things over—not only ourselves but also our partners, our kids, and all manner of situations in which we find ourselves. And it's never enough. We think something is missing, so we add to it measure after measure—more money, one more degree, another morsel of something.

And if after a while we have the semblance of "enough," then quite often we direct our creative power toward maintaining the packaging. The problem has evolved from adequately covering something over to keeping the secret that the original situation was ever disguised. Should we be surprised when defensiveness, guilt, or shame arises? The true condition or situation is probably something quite human—maybe sadness or hurt—but when we try to change it into something else, then we need to place all our energy into maintaining the cover, and little or no energy goes into helping the original situation. And what happens when whole groups of people, even whole nations, make maintaining the glitzy wrapping on their empty boxes a priority?

We might be satisfied for a short while, admiring the pretty boxes under the tree, but it wears thin pretty quickly. Christmas morning eventually arrives, and we find out that there is no Santa Claus. Events in our life—getting laid off from our job, experiencing illness, suffering loss—will inevitably make us aware that the wrapping cannot serve as armor. So too on the larger scale of communities and societies—great towers toppling, hunger and disease running rampant, rage and terror spinning round and round in a world caught up in lots of different wrappings. We're brought to the despair of ground zero—our empty boxes. Wrapping empty boxes, we never fully see the riches inside. We never taste the sweetness of what is. The only real gift is the one presented to us. It's the gift of life as it is. It is a gift always being offered us. How do we receive it?

PRACTICE

Pause in this moment to just look around the room in which you are reading this book. Look to right and to the left. Notice the objects, the people, and the space between the objects. Receive the environment by opening to all that comes to you through your senses: a dog barking, the cars going by, the light through the window, the air across your face. Try to not leave anything out. Let whatever comes into your awareness simply arise. Speak aloud the name of whatever you notice that is offering itself to you and/or to others. For example, the sunlight on your face, the air entering your nostrils, the solid ground under your feet, the light from the lamp overhead, oxygen from the trees, the jittery stomach . . . What do you see? A dirty sock your partner left on the floor? A dirty dish in the sink? The unpaid bill? Let it all in. Really see it. Notice your reactions. And let those in as well.

Now ask yourself what *you* are offering to both others and to yourself. For example, offering your attention by listening to another person speaking, overseeing a child at play, holding the door open for a person behind you entering a store, giving yourself care by savoring a hot cup of tea, breathing out carbon dioxide for the plants in your house to take in and turn into oxygen. Now look around the room and name something that does *not* offer itself to you personally. Is there anything?

The previous exercise brings to light something that we don't necessarily see most of the time—the natural abundance that is life itself and that is constantly offering itself to nourish beings. Much of life is invisible. Do we see a plant grow? We tend the little plants even though we don't see progress immediately. We nurture their potential with water and sunlight, but, in truth, there's no guarantee they'll grow. We are surrounded with what sustains life, and yet, for most of us, unless we purposely take the time to cultivate the eye and heart to let it in, we don't see it. Do you see the billions of microbes feeding on and nurturing the skin on your hands that hold this book? Think about it for a moment. Think of all that is giving forth from us and coming to us in this very moment that we have absolutely no sense of.

No matter who you are, no matter what you have done or have not done in your life, no matter what you think about yourself or what others think about you, the fact is, you breathe. And because you breathe, your breath feeds into and sustains innumerable life forces. Too often, because we don't see how connected we already are, we take action that is harmful. We peddle our way through life with our wheels out of kilter. The practice of Dana, of Giving and Receiving, begins by revealing to us what veils those human qualities at the core of our hearts and minds. So, it's the act of giving itself that brings up the mind of generosity. And it is the mind of generosity, which is also referred to as "magnanimous mind," that places us on the first stepping-stone of deep hope.

Magnanimous Mind

> As for what is called magnanimous mind, this mind is like the great mountains or like the great ocean; it is not biased or contentious mind. Carrying half a pound, do not take it lightly; lifting forty pounds should not seem heavy. Although drawn by the voices of spring, do not wander over spring meadows; viewing the fall colors, do not allow your heart to fall. The four seasons cooperate in a single scene; regard light and heavy with a single eye. On this single occasion you must write the word "great." You must know the word "great." You must learn the word "great."
> —Dogen Zenji, *Dogen's Pure Standards for the Zen Community*

The inherent human capacity of giving and receiving turns us toward what can be described as "magnanimous mind"— spacious and full, containing everything. In the Buddhist teaching, magnanimous mind is sometimes compared to a mountain—huge, standing firm, bearing witness to everything:

seasons, clouds, storms, wind. It is also compared to the ocean—vast, open, expansive, and inclusive of everything. It includes all that we want and all that we don't want, and for this reason, is also courageous mind. It's present and attentive. With equanimity, it lets in whatever arises. It doesn't measure but rather receives all phenomena with openness and a sense of possibility.

Magnanimous mind is also sometimes expressed as "not-knowing mind," for it only arises when we've leaned into and released the parameters of our fixed view of ourselves and the world. This is not a philosophical or ideological endeavor but a courageous and often difficult commitment to let go of deeply held assumptions and beliefs. Who are we when we cease holding on to our opinions and beliefs about "for and against," "good or bad," "right or wrong," and so forth? Zen master Sengcan reminds us: "Do not search for the truth; only cease to cherish opinions."[1]

Parental Mind

Parental mind is what follows naturally when we have moved from narrow to wider vision, including more and more of the world. It's not just about us and our loved ones; it's about wanting the best for the world. Our circle of care has widened to include more and more of life. We do this naturally for those close to us but perhaps not so readily for a stranger or for someone we don't know. Even less so for those with whom we have difficulty. Anyone who cares for young children knows what it means to want the best for the child. The baby wakes in the middle of the night crying with hunger; the parent crawls out of bed and sees that the baby is fed. As a young mother, I simply wanted presents under the tree for my baby daughter.

Joyful Mind

The *Flower Ornament Scripture*, a famous text of Mahayana Buddhism, contains a compelling discussion of the practice of joy. "So what is this practice of giving joy?" asks the scripture. "It is given by magnanimous givers."[2]

Freedom from the boundaries of self brings true joy. This is not the usual kind of joy we think of when we get something we want or have worked for. It's more like what is called "sympathetic joy," when we take delight in another's happiness (as in parental mind). When we practice the Paramita of Giving and Receiving, by giving, relinquishing, we create joyful mind for ourselves. Joyful mind emerges from experiencing others' joy as our own. It knows no jealousy, no winners, and no losers. Empty boxes overflow in abundance.

Living Hope:
Transformative Practice of Giving and Receiving

Bringing our attention, intention, effort, and energy into the practice of giving and receiving can be transformative. Magnanimous mind leads to parental mind. Joyous mind then arises of its own accord. It's not something we can force, but rather what is left when, if even for a moment, the circle begins to stretch to include more and more. Our hearts begin to open more and more. We begin by consciously calling forth a mind that expands to include more of what we normally fail to see or appreciate. We do this frequently throughout the day until it becomes automatic. (Note: this practice does not take extra time; it only takes our intention and effort.) We then meet whatever has come into our awareness with openness and curiosity, allowing it to be as it is. If you stick with this practice long enough, you will find yourself starting to care for what you encounter in a way that acknowledges its function (parental mind, the mind of love).

When we engage in whatever presents itself, the mind of generosity arises. When, even for a few moments, we widen our narrow circle into awareness of the fullness of what life is offering up to us, and when we take action out of that awareness, we experience a freedom that can only be described as joyful mind.

What We Can Give

We always have something to give. Sometimes, all we can give is the gift of ourselves—our intention to be fully present and respectful, to meet others with openness. We can give our story or listen to another's story. We can give our fearlessness, encouragement, or silent support of all kinds. We can give our stability or effort. We can give speaking and listening from the heart.

We can also practice giving to ourselves with an open, magnanimous mind. Putting ourselves first is sometimes the generous thing to do, but without magnanimous mind, it's self-indulgence. This is a tricky one and not always easy to discern. But, from the perspective of Zen, all giving begins with ourselves. We can give ourselves the opportunity to be fully present in the experience of anger, aware of our clenching teeth and tensing muscles. We can give ourselves the experience of the pounding heart of fear. We can give ourselves the experience of the heavy body and tearful eyes of sadness. To open our heart and minds to our experience is a form of giving and receiving.

When we open to our experience in this way, we relinquish the boundaries, the holding on. Instead of drawing our circle in closer and tighter, we can lean into its circumference and question deeply held requirements in the self's thinking about how it should be or needs to be. This is also generosity. When we give ourselves the gift of relinquishing that requirement, we open up the space to turn toward the experience of what's happening. And we open to those experiences. This is generosity—openness, acceptance, allowing.

As with anything that is meant to be inspirational, our minds can turn the Paramita of Giving and Receiving into an ideal, such that we try to become someone who gives and receives without any ideas about it. This is neither useful nor realistic. We cannot talk ourselves into having a constant experience of open, compassionate wisdom. We cannot force our way into experiencing the flow of giving and receiving. What we can do is earnestly look and listen. We can inquire, in a nonjudgmental way, "What is my experience of giving? What is my experience of receiving?"

In this way, we can receive people and their stories, and even our own stories, with open arms, with compassion. We can receive them, openly and without judgment, but we don't have to believe them. We can acknowledge that we really don't want to agree to make dinner for next week, take on that task at work, or change the baby's diaper again, and then we can just do it (or not) and see what it teaches us. We don't have to be completely certain that it's the "right" thing to do. When the person on the street asks us for spare change, we can acknowledge our confusion and then just drop a coin (or not) into her hand and see what happens. This is what practice teaches us—always question, and never look for the answers. Just let them come forth and reveal themselves to us.

The Courage of Giving

If over time we make a serious effort to engage in giving, sooner or later we will find ourselves facing moments of resistance to the mind states of generosity. It's not a question of time or even resources, but the willingness to face and question the perceived gap between self and other—the gap that makes "thou" into "it." It is the courage to let go of that separation. What's going on in the ten feet between me and the person's extended hand asking for spare change? It's so easy and tempting to remain within our little perimeters of safety, to stay within those circles that are "socially acceptable." Our circles may feel safe and pleasant, but the place of feeling good may not be the place of self-inquiry and self-discovery—the place from which we can tap the spring of who we are. I recall hearing about an indigenous tribe where parents have the practice of whispering to their little children while they are sleeping, "May you become all that you are." What a brave thing for a parent to do. It takes courage to let our children, or anyone we love, become all that they are. Do we dare? Can we live with not already knowing who they are and just support their becoming? It takes courage to do it for our children, but also for ourselves. It takes great courage to allow us to be all that we are—now, here, in this place. Do we dare?

The Courage of Receiving

Many of us face the revealing experience that the act of receiving is as or more challenging than the act of giving. Many years ago when, as a beginner Zen student, I was assigned to be the cook for a retreat, I gave it my utmost effort to serve wholesome, tasty, and well-prepared food. At the end of the retreat, one of the senior students came to me and said, "Thank you for all your efforts. The food was wonderful." But rather than simply accepting her thanks with a simple "You're welcome" or "I'm glad you enjoyed it," I remember feeling very uncomfortable—my body grew rigid, and I felt tongue-tied and just plain awkward. I mumbled something about it not really being special and pointed out some of the mistakes I made. My response, however, wasn't to be missed, for the senior student immediately looked me in the eye and asked, "What is standing in the way of your receiving my thanks?" Her question was one I practiced with for many years before I was able to realize that I often responded to compliments in that way, and that what was standing in the way of my receiving the gift was a sense of low self-worth and self-esteem. For some, receiving what's given is also tied to a belief that the gift is a form of recognition.

It's also interesting to reflect on our responses when we're given material gifts. When we're given the "perfect" gift, we may feel fully recognized by the giver, but sometimes the gift we receive may not seem so perfect. Even though we may not express it verbally, we may feel an inner rejection. Rejecting a gift because it isn't what we hoped for or doesn't reflect that the giver knows what will please us, rejects not just the gift but the spirit of giving that has come your way. It is the offering of the gift and not the gift itself that connects us to others.

And then there are the gifts that come from life itself. How do we receive an illness, a loss of a loved one, or a loss of a job or a position? These situations may not reveal themselves as gifts until we turn our attention toward what they might teach us. Often people who have suffered life's blows will later share that all that they learned from the experience was a great gift. Exploring what comes up for us in these types of situations can be revealing and is the work of practicing with the Paramita of Giving and Receiving.

STUDENT SHARING

One of my students shared the following account:

When I think of practicing generosity I think of the word *we*. I've come to understand that practicing generosity requires both giver and receiver. Sometimes the lines blur. The receiver is practicing generosity by receiving. The giver gives, but also receives. We do it together.

A couple of weeks ago, I had a dizzy spell, which froze me standing in the middle of the street. Along came a local insurance agent whose name I recognized from seeing it on the building where he works. He asked if he could help, and I said yes. I asked him to walk me to my car so I could retrieve my walking stick, which is what I needed. He told me I had made his day by letting him help me. He helped me in a skillful way by letting me direct him. I realized afterward that I had not been generous with myself. I had been feeling a bit off when I got out of the car and should've grabbed my walking stick.

Later on, I paid it forward. A clinic patient who has trouble walking needed a ride home. I stayed a little late and gave her and her walker a ride home. She gave me a great gift by letting me help. I often help people by being generous with my time but because of my disability, it is not often that I get to do something physical to help someone. I got to load and unload her walker and drive her home. We did it together.

The Neurobiology of Generosity

Another perspective on the transformative aspect of the practice of generosity is to think of it as creating a new habit that is triggered by changes in the brain. We interpret the world through a vast collection of neurons. Though they are always developing, they have the tendency to settle into habitual ways of firing given particular stimuli. For me, the smell of coffee might be pleasing, setting off pleasant memories and perhaps causing my mouth to water. For another person, it may trigger feelings of distaste or even an upset stomach. Most of us know about this aspect of the brain. But from the perspective of the Paramita of Giving and Receiving, it has even more significance because it suggests that we can train the brain to respond in certain ways. By engaging in the practice of giving, we can slowly shift our neuronal association from "me" to "we"—transitioning from the restrictions of the self-centered dream we've been constantly maintaining, to moment-by-moment opening to the interconnectedness of all beings everywhere. Scientific studies have made it clear that our brains remain plastic throughout life—so why not turn that potential toward the practice and experience of giving and receiving?

Open Wide Our Narrow Hand to Receive and to Give

Clench your fist. Take a close look at it. Notice the effort it takes to hold the hand tightly closed in this manner. Then relax into allowing the fingers to open, and see that the palm has become free and open to give as well as to receive.

The first paramita encourages us to first say yes. Say yes to life. There is no hope without first saying yes. Hopelessness shouts no. Hope utters yes. This paramita invites us to stop, look, and listen to the subtlest and often hidden offerings that are presented to us moment by moment. And to be honest, as I write these words, I'm asking myself, "How can the father in a war-torn country, cradling the dead body of his infant child killed by a bomb, find even the tiniest hidden gift presenting itself in that moment?" This is the world before us now. This is what greets us over our morning coffee. What do we do? The answer to this question is different for each of us, but it always begins with our willingness to bear witness to the event, even though it may be painful. For one person, a response may simply be pausing and letting the pictures and story in to their full attention and to then take a deep breath in and out, sending heartfelt thoughts of well-being: "May you be safe; may you find peace." For another person, it may be sending a donation to an aid group working in the area. The important point here is that, even before we attempt to engage in a generous gesture, we intentionally turn our awareness toward receiving

—receiving our immediate experience, purposely bringing our attention to the ordinary objects, people, and events around us. This is the kind of present-moment basis that is necessary if we want to consciously try to cultivate broad, open, magnanimous mind; caring, nurturing, parental mind; or free and joyful mind. Even though we may only experience these mind states slightly or not at all, the power of our intention and the energy we put forth in effort resonate deep within and begin loosening the hold of our constrictions. This last point is the most important part of the practice to keep in mind because this loosening requires letting go in the face of fear. Opening to whatever finds its way into our life can be frightening, especially when we've come to rely on thinking or behaving in ways that try to keep certain experiences out. However, we come to learn that restricting what we let in, rejecting whatever conditions find their way into our lives, robs us of all that sustains us as well. Of course, it's easy to write these words here. It is much more difficult to carry out the practice in the face of our deep-seated habits of closure. Difficult, but possible—for we have a deep intelligence within that is there to serve us.

PRACTICE

Expand intentional awareness. As you're holding this book in your hands, turn your eyes to the right until they land on an object. It can be a pencil, a sock on the floor, a crumb on the table—the simpler, the better. Don't pick and choose, simply receive what enters into your vision awareness. Now make that object your focus of attention. Allow your awareness to include things you haven't noticed before— receive the shape of the pencil, the frayed thread on the sock, the indentation of the big toe. Try it on a few other objects in the room. If you're riding public transportation, try resting your eyes on someone's shoe. Now expand this intentional awareness to listening and spend a few moments with that. Then expand it to all five senses. As you become more comfortable with this practice, try doing it in the office, on the bus, at a traffic light, in a restaurant, or waiting in line at the grocery store. The places to practice the early steps of this paramita are endless, and the more you do it, the easier it will be. In fact, in time, you'll find your mind moving in the direction of generous awareness with less and less effort.

Thirty-day practice: giving and receiving. Every morning when you first wake up, bring to mind something you receive and say it aloud. For example: "I receive fresh clean air to breathe." "I receive the smell of fresh coffee." "I receive the solid floor under my bare feet." Write it down. Then, every evening just before you close your eyes to go to sleep, say something you have given during the day. For example: "I let a person go ahead of me at the train station." "I gave myself a few moments of rest during lunch." "I listened to my coworker sharing his stress." Write it down. The next morning, repeat the previous incidents from your list and add one more. Do the same for the evening exercise. By the end of the thirty days, you will have recited thirty new incidents of receiving and thirty new incidents of giving.

The Gift of Listening

Writer Diane Ackerman noticed that, while working as a volunteer manning the phones of a suicide prevention telephone hotline, listening sometimes felt like "auditory braille"—a listening so active and engaged it was almost tactile. She describes this active listening as "echolocation," sending out "small reconnoitering sounds—a leading question, perhaps— and wait[ing] to hear in what shape and from where it echoes back." I find her description of listening to be a wonderful doorway to the experience of listening as a kind of gift:

> Listening athletically, with one's whole attention, one hears the sighs, the sniffling, the loud exhalations, the one-beat-longer-than-normal pause before a difficult or taboo word, the voice-falls of misgiving, the whittling of worry, the many diphthongs of grief, the heaving tongue of drunkenness, the piled ingots of guilt, the quiet screeching of self-blame, the breathlessness of fear, the restless volcano of panic, the fumings of stifled rage, the staccato spasms of frustration, the sidestepping anger of the "yes, but"-ers, the tumbling ideas of the developmentally disabled, the magic dramas of the hallucinator, the idea shards of the psychotic, the harrowed tones of the battered, the bleak deadpan of the hopeless, the pacing of the ambivalent, the entrenched gloom of depression, the distant recesses of loneliness, the anxiousness that is like a wringing of the hands.[3]

As we see in Ackerman's beautiful evocation of all the tones and valences of speech she experienced with the suicidal, when we listen as if life were on the line—which in truth it always is—listening appears as a gift.

PRACTICE

You may be familiar with several of the suggested practices below, but in the spirit of widening awareness, I encourage you to take a few moments before and after you've done each activity to pause and bear witness. For example, if you have decided that you will water the plant on your front porch every day as you leave your home, notice what's going on with you before you begin to water. If it's a busy, rushed day, or you're running late, what's your state of mind and body? Give yourself a few moments, a few breaths. This kind of check-in doesn't take a lot of time. It just takes significant intention. Then, just pick up the watering can and water. When you finish watering, check in again. What comes up?

Pay it forward. This is an old-time favorite practice of giving, one I find simple but powerful. Every time someone does something for you, pass on a similar deed to someone else within twenty-four hours. For example, if someone lets you go ahead of them getting on a bus, make a vow that you will do the same for someone else within twenty-four hours. And when you forget, and perhaps remember later, think back to where your intention to carry it forward got lost. Remember, none of the practices are intended to cause guilt. Guilt is just something that the self adds on. We're trying to wake up to patterns of thinking and acting with openness and curiosity. The power of this practice is that it heightens our attention to what we are receiving and encourages us to give in simple ways.

Here are some simple daily practices:

- Water a plant that looks like it could use a drink, even if you don't own it.
- Pick up some trash or litter you find as you walk along the street.
- If you bring something for yourself to eat or drink at a meeting, bring a little extra to share with others.
- Pay the toll for the car behind you in the "cash" lane of a toll station.
- At a busy intersection, give another car the right to pass.
- When waiting for a parking spot, give the space that just opened up in front of you to the person waiting behind you.

- Give someone who you find difficult to listen to your full attention for at least sixty seconds. (This is a particularly powerful practice in developing the Paramita of Practicing Patience, which we'll discuss in chapter 4 of this book.)
- Give someone the benefit of the doubt.
- Take in your neighbor's barrels.

Opening to Receive

This morning I watered a plant on my desk that I'd been ignoring in the busyness of writing this book. As I took a moment to explore the crack between popping out words about gratitude and actually finding it within the reality of life presenting itself before me, I watched over the next few minutes as the plant slowly began to sit upright. "Thank you," it said. And I said, "Thank *you*, for you have given me a few moments to connect with what's right in front of me."

In some cultures, bowing is a way of expressing gratitude. Often at Buddhist centers, where bowing is frequent, newcomers feel uncomfortable because they are not used to bowing as an expression of gratitude. But I like to tell people to think of bowing as a simple gesture: placing hands together, receiving with openness and possibility, and inviting our hearts to be open and accepting. I often remind people that when we bow, we are bowing *with*, not *to*.

We live in a culture in which we are conditioned to think that more is better. It's surprising to me how easy it is to add one more thing to buy, do, or learn in the belief that our life will be richer, fuller, or more meaningful. The Paramita of Giving and Receiving helps us to discover that it's not so much what we add but what we take away that reveals what is always there to sustain and nurture us. So, purposely cultivating a practice of simplifying is very useful.

PRACTICE

Choose a small area of your environment that you come into contact with every day. For example, the spot in your bathroom where you place your toothbrush, toothpaste, or dental floss, the place where you place your keys and wallet, or the space you keep your favorite drinking cup. Make this space your "nothing special" altar. When we think of altars, we may assume that they are made to give homage to something or someone special to us, and that the objects should also be "special." But this practice asks us to dip into the everydayness of reality and honor it all. Give yourself the opportunity to receive the specialness of an inexpensive, cracked cup or a used-up tube of toothpaste. The important point is that it's simple, ordinary, and not cluttered. Let there be plenty of space between the objects.

Make this your altar of gratitude. Every time you brush your teeth, make something to drink, or put your keys down, pause to really look at and take in the object. All of it. For example, when you hold the cup in your hand, feel its shape, its weight, and its temperature. Consider the many lives that brought you this cup—the workers who made it and the people who transported it, each of them having their own lives. Consider what the earth gave forward to produce the cup. These considerations are endless. As we say in our meal chant at the Zen center: "Innumerable labors brought us this food. We should know how it comes to us."

These are just a few suggestions to get you started. The key is to first widen your awareness to include anything that comes into your experience. At the same time, widen your awareness to recognize and give thanks to what you receive. Then, just make the effort to give and notice what comes up when you resist and when you just open up. Let this practice find its way into the nooks and crannies of your daily living. Don't make it special and don't try to set aside time for just doing it. As you engage in the Paramita of Meditating, which we'll explore in chapter 6, you'll find that you are able to stop and be quiet in the cracks between the activities of your busy life. And in those cracks, you'll find that the most ordinary events and objects are offering themselves to you. And there will be times when you find yourself simply engaging in the natural reciprocity where there is no one giving—no gift, no receiver. We can't *try* to do this. Rather, it is a natural evolution as we engage in the above practices. And we do it over and over, since we know that the opening and closing of our awareness is a natural part of being human.

STUDENT SHARING

Several of my students shared the following accounts:

- Visiting a very ill neighbor, I entered a space filled with the odor of sickness and saw the mess of an unkept house. I dreaded it. But going into his bedroom, I turned my mind to his condition, and I genuinely turned my attention to him, how he was doing, and what he wanted to say. Every time my mind got distracted by the smell, I simply turned my attention back to listening, hearing the words. And when I did that, I discovered all sorts of interesting things that we could share about nature shows on TV, the hummingbird nesting outside the window, and I came to find out we both had relatives who lived in Southern California. . . . I went to my neighbor's house to give him my time and he gave me his wonderful story.

- A coworker who I have resistance to was doing a short presentation this week. Instead of spinning my usual negative thoughts, I tried giving her my fullest attention —eyes, ears, mind, all the senses I could muster. This focus, which took effort and intention, seemed to leave no room in my mind for judgment and also no need; a benevolent feeling toward her and others has stayed with me throughout the week.

- For me, it's always a question of what am I leaving out, which takes the form of thoughts about "how it should be" replacing the truth of "how it is." This is especially true at the busy hospital where I work and I am always struggling to catch up with appointments and juggle a system that doesn't easily "connect the dots." I often find myself in a dance between grumbling and complaining and simply including what is. But when I pause in the middle of grumbling and ask myself, "What am I leaving out?" I find my circle widens to include the patients, the overworked staff, the computer not working correctly, the system that really doesn't work . . .

- As a caregiver, I've found the most challenging thing for me is to meet the person I'm working with where and how they are at a given moment. Even though I've trained for this, it's not very easy and it's always a moving target. But what I've found is that just being there letting go of my need to *do* something is most helpful for both of us. Sometimes, I just don't have it in me to *do* anything, so I just sit there. I've come to appreciate the power of giving this presence.

3

Taking Skillful Action

SHILA PARAMITA

The salvation of this human world lies nowhere
else than in the human heart, in the human
power to reflect, in human modesty, and in
human responsibility.
—Václav Havel, *The Art of the Impossible*

SHILA IS a Sanskrit word meaning "to cool" or "to calm."
It suggests that taking care with our actions is not intended to
become an eradication of human tendencies. Rather, to cool
or calm has a different connotation than to uproot or destroy.
Destructive intentions are quite heavy, and in all honesty, I don't
think we can ever eradicate those tendencies completely. The
Buddhist precepts serve as guideposts that help us recognize
where we cause suffering for ourselves and others through
carelessness, irresponsibility, and exploitive hurtful actions.
Engaging them in this paramita stimulates a recognition, you
might say "ownership," of the struggles we face as human
beings. On the one hand, we are our "brother's keeper," and
on the other hand, we may be afraid of our brother, hate him,
or not even know him. What would Taking Skillful Action
mean in the midst of these varying kinds of relationships?[1]

The Eight Precepts of Taking Skillful Action

The Buddhist precepts came about originally as rules to govern the community of monks and nuns who gathered about the Buddha. They included very precise instructions such as not handling money, not eating certain foods, and not touching people of the opposite sex. They were intended to support the monks and nuns in their monastic practice. Later, as Buddhism spread into lay communities, the precepts were broadened to include people who had not undertaken such austere forms of practice. Today, the precepts are also taken by people who live their lives driving the freeways, doing time in prisons, changing baby diapers. For some, the precepts are viewed as a preliminary step in becoming a Buddhist practitioner. For some they are taken only for the duration of a meditation retreat. In the Zen tradition, taking the precepts is made formal in the ceremony of *Jukai* in which a student is initiated as a Lay Buddhist Practitioner.

1. I take up the way of speaking truthfully.
2. I take up the way of speaking of others from openness and possibility.
3. I take up the way of meeting others on equal ground.
4. I take up the way of cultivating a clear mind.
5. I take up the way of taking only what is freely given and giving freely of all that I can.
6. I take up the way of engaging in intimacy respectfully and with an open heart.
7. I take up the way of letting go of anger.
8. I take up the way of supporting life.

How the Precepts Work

The precepts function on several levels. First, they serve as warning lights—sometimes like a stoplight that reminds us to put on the brakes rather than hurtle forward into hurtful action or like a lighthouse beacon that warns sailors that they are entering dangerous waters and keeps them on course. Second, they encourage a mental attitude of taking action that is supportive rather than harmful. Third, when, perhaps after long practice with the precepts, clarity arises as to their wisdom, the boundaries of self and others fall away, and our actions flow naturally out of selfless activity—this is living an ethical or virtuous life.

When it functions as a stoplight, a given precept simply reminds us to say no before moving on. However, this no is not meant as a rejection or a denial of our intention but rather as a reminder to refrain from what might be habitual reactions and patterns. Think of the no as creating a space for us to explore alternative action.

Just as in our practice of the Paramita of Giving and Receiving, the Paramita of Taking Skillful Action does not follow a linear progression. Rather, we find it's a constant turning from self-centeredness to life centeredness. It's an ongoing practice that embraces intention, effort, and courage. Once more, it's not always completely clear. The Zen tradition offers codes of moral conduct as boundaries in which we can do the deep work of studying the self. We look at and question our intentions and do what we need to do to cultivate clarity and awareness so that we are as cognizant as possible of the many various and dynamic conditions that comprise any situation.

A Place Called Home

The practice of virtuous or wise actions begins with our deciding what we will return to no matter what life brings our way—joy, happiness, sadness, sorrow, or sickness. Buddhist teachings call this "taking refuge." A place of refuge is a place of security and sanctuary, but more than just a haven of safety, it is also where we find the strength and energy to support us in living a happy life. We begin by taking refuge in what are called the Three Precious Jewels, or the Three Treasures: Buddha, Dharma, and Sangha.[2] Taking refuge also means returning to ourselves, our true nature, as awakened human beings who, without exception, possess open hearts and minds. We may feel that we or others don't have such a nature, but that's only because we have forgotten what's true. And every so often it pokes through like a flash of lightening in the dark, and we remember. Then, quite often, we again forget. So, taking the vow to return to the Three Treasures is a way of helping and supporting ourselves, a way to remember and return to our refuge. We vow to take refuge in:

- The deepest wisdom and compassion within each of us—that which is at the core of what we are.
- Understanding and living with the teachings, which help us bring forth compassion and wisdom.
- The community of all beings and our interconnection with everything, not just on this planet but in all the billions of galaxies astronomy has revealed.

Next, we take a vow that serves to remind us of our intention of how we want to live our life. We vow to:

- Avoid all action in body, speech, and mind that creates suffering. This is a vow of restraint.
- Take action that creates true happiness. This is a vow of awareness of what we can do specifically.
- Take action that includes others in our hearts and minds. This is a vow to keep in mind that our happiness and others' happiness are interconnected—that when we reach out to help others, we help ourselves.

Finally, we take up the vow for more specific actions through eight additional precepts that are sometimes called the "grave" precepts. It's good to keep in mind though, that we don't mean "grave" as in grim or somber but rather as weighty, significant, or profound. The primary function of these precepts is to help us look deep within ourselves, to find what veils our deepest qualities as human beings.

If we take refuge in the precepts, they will help bring down the walls of separation with which we have been living, revealing our connection to loved ones and enemies alike. They reveal our connection not just to people and animals but to the blades of grass under our feet, the river filled with plastic bottles and chemicals, the delicate sway of ecological balance, and our leaders who bring us in and out of war and declare our nation's friends or foes. They reveal the ways in which we fall into vicious cycles of thinking and acting, causing suffering to ourselves and others. The precepts are never intended to make us view these actions as moral defects but rather as the root source of suffering. To practice with the precepts is to begin opening a passage through which we can be free of that suffering.

I Take Up the Way of Speaking Truthfully

This precept encourages us to consider carefully the very nature of deception, and by doing so, it directs us to what is real and true. What causes us to engage in deception? Taking up the way of speaking truthfully can help us begin to explore our conditioning and the delusory beliefs that prevent us from engaging honestly and wholly in the experience of living. In a world that seems so deeply steeped in all levels and types of deception, sifting through our own forms of deception is not such an easy task. But by turning our awareness toward uncovering the ways in which we delude others, we can come to recognize a deeper betrayal of ourselves and of truth itself. One of my students rephrased this precept in this way: "I take up the way of honestly facing the distrust, uncertainty, and fear that propels my tongue to be disloyal to the truth of this moment."

When we begin observing with the spirit of open inquiry how we are deceiving, we may be surprised at how often we wander from speaking truthfully. Not telling the truth can range from a harmless fib such as cutting off a telephone solicitor by saying, "I'm just on my way out the door," when in truth what we want is to sit down to dinner, to harmful lies to deflect blame and suspicion from our own actions. We can sprinkle part truth with part lie, or we can try to create truth by presenting what we wish were true as if it were fact. Sometimes we stay silent, failing to speak out when we should and thus engaging in silent deception. Sometimes we lie to prevent others from feeling hurt, like when we lie to a child about something we know will be very painful or when we lie to keep bad news to ourselves so we don't worry loved ones. Sometimes we keep silent and lie by omission, taking the route of indifference. Some of us anguish over the simplest fib, while some of us have learned to distrust truth to such an extent that lying has become the habitual way of reacting to events. And there are many variations of deception in between. Finally, deception isn't limited to what we tell others; it also includes what we tell ourselves.

PRACTICE

Becoming aware of untruthful situations. Begin paying close attention to how and in what situations you hedge on the truth or tell outright untruths. Also notice times when you keep silent when it might be better to speak up. Silence can also be an untruth. After you become familiar with your particular style of not being truthful, notice what might be under it. In other words, is there something you are trying to hold on to or protect? An image of yourself? Let yourself experience the full range of emotions, thoughts, and feelings that arise with the idea of being honest in situations in which you have noticed yourself being dishonest. Over time, as you continue tracking your habits of speech, take a chance and speak the truth. See what happens. You might try by limiting your inquiry to specific situations where you have noticed a habit of engaging in deception, but you may also keep it broad. The key is to *listen* closely to yourself as you speak—at work, at breakfast, at the supermarket, in the doctor's office. Notice the volume, tone, and expression of your voice. Facial expressions and body stance also speak volumes. Bring your awareness here as well. There is no specific place to do this part of the practice. Just do it. If you look for ways you deceive and keep an open ear to deceptive words, you might be surprised to find quite a few. Remember, however, that the judge or inner critic is not invited into this self-inquiry.

Deepening the inquiry. Once you've identified a few typical situations, you're ready to inquire a little deeper. Now, at whatever point you realize you've engaged in a deception, turn your awareness inward and feel your body. Are there any sensations like heart pounding, dry mouth, blushing, or a sinking feeling? See if that sensation wants to name itself, perhaps with the word *guilt, shame,* or *fear* or another word. Don't demand an answer. Just invite it. Notice what sorts of thoughts are present and notice if they string together in a story line. What is that story? "I'm bad. I'll never get this. I'm found out. What will they think? How can I cover this?" Are you thinking of further deceptions to cover the last deception? The mind might be racing pretty fast at this point. It's not necessary to catch all the thoughts. Just one. Then just repeat it to yourself. "Having a thought that . . ." You've just spoken truthfully! Don't try to change anything. The purpose is to simply bring attention to what you're experiencing and be honestly in its presence.

If you do this for some time, over quite a few occasions, you'll begin to notice that the lens of your awareness grows sharper and more readily available. The beacon or stoplight goes on a lot more quickly as you find yourself engaging in a deception or feeling tempted to do so. One of my students reported that he felt he hardly ever communicated without deceiving in some way. When people begin to practice this precept, they're sometimes surprised at how often they engage in deceptive speech. This can be a difficult time, especially if the self-judging guilt mind takes over. But, relying on the Buddhist teachings, we meet the judging mind as we would any other thought/emotion/body reaction: Label. Feel. Breathe. Move on.

It is at this point that it is useful to engage the precept as a stop sign that says: "Stop before you proceed." Just to stop the action is not enough, however. Saying to yourself, "I'm not going to speak deception in this situation" is useful to a certain extent, of course, but leaving it there will not help you proceed into a deeper understanding of the falseness of your beliefs. So, stop the action but then begin the inquiry.

The inquiry begins within the pause. It is right here that the deception is unveiled by delving further into the experience. It is important to keep in mind the spirit of a Zen riddle that encourages the process of open inquiry: "What's the worst thing that could happen if I spoke the truth here?" The question is put forth but then released. It's as if you send out a probe into the darkness, without knowing what, if anything, you will find. It is the questioning that has the power here, not the answer.

You cannot predict the timetable or number of times you will need to go through a certain pattern with this inquiring orientation. But you can be confident that, eventually, and when the time is right—or, more accurately, when you are ready—an insight will begin to emerge. You will know it in your gut, but you will also feel it and breathe it in its complete presence.

A student of mine, who is a nurse, worked with this precept for several months, noticing on many occasions that she was engaging in deception by trying to keep silent. Eventually she began to have a sense that what she was trying to keep silent was the belief that if she said what was on her mind, she would be rejected. She allowed herself to experience the rising and falling feeling of this anticipated rejection in her body, whenever it came up, opening for as long as she could to it. At first, just a moment or two, and over time, longer and longer periods of time—pounding heart, closed chest, just breathing in and out. Over and over, she paused in open stillness, allowing the sensation labeled "rejection" to rise and fall away—moving, changing, in constant flux.

I Take Up the Way of Speaking of Others from Openness and Possibility

This precept invites us to question deeply the assumptions and beliefs that find their way into our comments as we speak disparagingly of others. One of my students worded it this way: "When I talk about others, who is speaking? Fear and shame inside push critical words outside. I vow to pause so the distress in the mind and body can speak." This precept also addresses the unspoken faultfinding conversations we have within our thoughts.

In a broader view, this precept invites us to not only speak of others but to also *meet* others with openness and possibility. It is true that speaking disparagingly aloud about another person can have far-reaching effects, but at a deeper level, the mind that has frozen its view of another, even if the thoughts are unspoken, is not capable of being open and awake. It has been my experience that some of our most deeply entrenched faultfinding is for those with whom we have the closest relationships—especially the critical views children hold of their parents and parents have of their children. I am not speaking here of those criticisms we may pass through as children and teenagers, but the static perceptions we hang on to as adults.

We can begin to thaw these frozen views of others by asking simple questions such as, "How do I think they should be?" or "What do I think they should do?" Then follow with the questions, "How are they?" or "What do they do?" It becomes clear that to speak of others with openness and possibility, we must first meet them where they are. Bearing witness to others in this way takes a great deal of courage because oftentimes we feel safer when secured behind our established views about who other people are and what they do.

Studying the ways in which we discuss the faults of others can reveal much about the ways in which we protectively encircle our worldviews in general. When subtle self-serving intentions are added onto the words we speak about other people, we create distance both from them and from ourselves.

By creating this separation, we encourage specialness of me. Feelings of inadequacy, imperfection, fear, and shame may be temporarily assuaged, but they are only pushed aside to reappear at another time. We deeply harm others when we speak of them in degrading ways, and we harm ourselves as well because we don't make space for acceptance, compassion, and generosity in our life.

PRACTICE

Exploring your reactions. A good way to explore this precept, including how to use it for everyday decision-making, is by trying out the following exercise for a week or two. Remember, there's no timetable or race to be won. You may find that you only get to point one. That's fine. Once you bring up the intention to explore your reactions in this way, the observer is activated and over time will become stronger.

Stop, take inventory. Take one week to begin noticing the obvious and subtle ways in which you talk about others—overtly, surreptitiously, to yourself, to others? Keep a journal.

Look, focus in. Choose one or two specific ways in which you talk about others, noticing where and under what conditions you do it.

Listen. Hear your words as you speak in these particular situations. Pay close attention to the tone of your voice, noticing what happens to your voice and to your word choice when you stop sharing information and begin discussing faults. For example: "Harry again didn't do what I asked him—he can't be depended on." Is your tone implying fact or is it finger-pointing? Is it snide, sarcastic? Is it neutral, just relaying an observation?

Experience. Notice if there is any emotional charge present. Your body sensations are a good indicator here. If you're feeling some tightness or other discomfort, there's a good chance that your comments are fueled by some negative feelings. Continue looking, listening, and experiencing in this way until you clarify the emotion. For example, you might notice there is really some jealousy fueling your comment.

Repeat. Repeat your communication, looking for a way to convey it more neutrally. With the sentence about Harry, for example, you might change it to: "It's been my experience that Harry doesn't always carry through on tasks." Notice the difference in the words and in how you feel saying them. In the first sentence, you are freezing your perception of Harry into a static entity. From a Zen perspective, this perception can only be false. In the second sentence, you are just communicating behavior you have witnessed with Harry. One closes off to the continual opening and creation of a "Harry." The other allows him to be as he is. And of course, what we close off is not just Harry but our openness to him and to much more. It closes off our mind to the impermanence out of which life is always re-creating itself. So, speaking of faults is harmful not just to the other person but also to ourselves, to our aliveness.

Respond. What kind of response suggests itself from this new statement about your experience? Just because your coworker, partner, or child hasn't followed through on tasks in the past, do you stop giving him tasks altogether? Or do you keep giving them to him with the knowledge that he is capable of change and if given the opportunity he could follow through? I once received the Zen teaching, "A so-called fault is a weak place where character can change." If we don't invest ourselves in allowing a weakness to strengthen, then we have not fully experienced the practice of this precept.

Deepening the inquiry. Once we've really engaged this precept, we have the opportunity to more deeply explore the driving power behind our speech. Ask yourself, "What am I adding on to the information I am conveying?" Again, be sure to listen carefully to your tone and words. For example, if you hear someone yell at his friend, you could say to yourself, "That man is mean." But if you allow yourself to simply rest in just this, you would say to yourself, "That man is yelling at his friend." By simply stating the man's behavior, you haven't found fault, nor have you frozen "what he is." This precept helps us reveal what we add to facts, perhaps mixing a bit of assumption or projection into what is observably true.

Finding fault with others also extends to larger situations. We find fault with the government, the schools, the "establishment." Every day we're presented with trivial and not-so-trivial information about the world through the media, social networks, other people, and our own perceptions. How are we to sift out the true from the untrue? How does this relate to blame and to what we get out of blaming? It's easy to point fingers at what's wrong in the world. Even though it may be a fact that many of our leaders' actions are not in the best interest of the world's population, who are we serving when we blame? By blaming, we relieve ourselves of the responsibility of taking action ourselves, believing it's someone else's responsibility, someone else's "fault." Again, it seems that our blame and negative speech can say more about ourselves than about others.

Evaluating your remarks. Think about the following process of investigating what speaking disparagingly can tell you about yourself. Ask yourself: "What does talking about this person in this way do for my own self-image?" For example, do you feel better about yourself in some way when you fault someone else? Ask, "How does speaking of this person's behavior as faults serve me? Why do I really do it?" Does it justify your own behavior? Do you feel more accepted by the people you're with? Does it make you feel important? In other words, by saying another has faults, does it make you feel that you're not alone in your perceived faults? Or perhaps it makes you feel superior: "I'm bad, but he's worse. He's bad, and I'm good." Either way, our speech can be a way of avoiding the deep belief of being *less than*.

Now try seeing yourself in the other person and honestly try to find examples in yourself when you have been like the person you are discussing. Change the statement, "Harry is undependable" to the question, "How am I undependable?" Watch for situations in which you may not follow through. In other words, look at your own behavior. The idea is to keep an open awareness about your behavior. Don't judge your behavior or even try to change it, although it may change quite naturally once you become aware of your actions. What is your experience now? How do you feel about this other person? About yourself? Perhaps you feel less judgmental of her, or perhaps you notice some guilt or some other feelings arise.

Now exercise the prohibitory aspect of the precept. Stop yourself from speaking disparagingly about Harry. Ask yourself, "If, right in this moment, I did not find fault with Harry, what's the worst thing that can happen?" Stay open. If any feelings, emotions, or bodily sensations arise, label them and rest with them, breathing in and out. This particular question brings us to the core of our behavior, and if we stick it out, we can find what fuels it. If you're in a group, make an attempt to stop yourself from talking about others by removing yourself from the group or biting your tongue. Stay open to your reactions without feeling compelled to act on them.

Now consider what your relationship with this person would be like if you simply acknowledged their behavior without finding fault with it.

STUDENT SHARING

Student: What about when we keep silent about a person? I don't mean like in lying, as we talked about in the speaking truthfully precept. But say for example I'm having coffee with some people from work and someone mentions how great a job a coworker is doing on a project, and I just keep silent because I don't agree with them. Is my silence a statement of sorts?

Diane: This reminds me of instructions many of us may have heard as children: "If you can't say something good about a person, don't say anything." My own feeling is that we can't get off the hook so easily if we truly want to engage in what's going on, but we need to question our intent in keeping silent. Sometimes silence would be the best course of action. If there's a lot being said, and you can't add any useful information, you may choose to remain silent. But sometimes silence can be louder than words. Saying nothing at the right time can speak volumes.

Student: What about the opposite of seeing others from the point of view of fault? I find that sometimes I will only praise certain people. Isn't this another way of freezing my perception of them?

Diane: Yes. A trickier version, but nevertheless this is the same thing. But remember, the practice is to reveal how we use faultfinding to solidify our self-identity.

Student: I'm wondering about your comments on the difference between speaking and thinking about another person's faults. Are you suggesting that there's no less harm in just thinking the thought as opposed to speaking it?

Diane: It's been my experience that if I can catch the thought, then I'm more likely able to do some of the practice with it. So, in that sense, there is a huge difference between thought and action. But as I mentioned earlier, the thought finds its way to the tongue with lightning speed, and there's all kinds of juicy "stuff" in between. Most of the time, we're not awake to what we're doing until we hear the words escape our lips (or get hit with the repercussions of our words).

I Take Up the Way of
Meeting Others on Equal Ground

> It is a terrible, an inexorable, law that one cannot
> deny the humanity of another without diminish-
> ing one's own; in the face of one's victim, one sees
> oneself.
> —James Baldwin, *Nobody Knows My Name*

This precept invites us to explore the subtle ways we use others as a yardstick to measure our self-worth by placing ourselves above or below them. It is sometimes worded, "Not Praising Self at the Expense of Others" or "Not Praising Yourself While Abusing Others." The previous precept explored the ways we demean others and ourselves by thinking and speaking of them from the perspective of faults. In this precept, we explore what prevents us from meeting others on equal ground. I do not mean equal talents, abilities, strengths, or weaknesses. Rather I mean equal as human beings. How do we move out of seeing relationships as a realm of competition with winners and losers? Another of my students has phrased it this way:

> Do I exist outside the realm of judgment and comparison
> with others? Do others exist when I spin in the realm of
> fantasy and belief? Insecurity, anger, and shame bar the
> way. I vow to let frozen breath, pounding heart, and
> churning stomach lead me through.

PRACTICE

Notice the ways you measure yourself against others. As with the other precepts, study your actions, words, body, and thoughts. You no doubt will find that you have certain favorite reactions, including some that are finely tuned for certain people and situations. Watch how your thoughts create a story about people rather than letting them reveal themselves. At some point, you'll begin to be able to catch yourself entering the story every now and again before you've fully committed yourself to it. When this happens, experience what it's like to engage without the story. This needn't be just with new people but also with your partner, your kids, or anyone you've known for a long time. Try meeting them as if for the first time—as strangers, just as in the last precept. Turn your attention to their physical characteristics. What is the color of their eyes? Look at their face as if you were seeing them for the first time. Listen to what they're saying and how they're saying it—the words, the pauses, and the voice intonation. This is not as difficult as it may seem. It's simply a matter of turning your attention toward what is in front of you, not what's in your head. No story, just what is.

I Take Up the Way of Cultivating a Clear Mind

Originally, this precept focused on the use of alcohol, but later it was expanded to include the use of other substances such as tranquilizers, hallucinogens, and so forth. Today, we can think of the subtler ways we turn from being present by using and abusing not only dramatically mind-altering drugs but also more subtle ones such as caffeine, cigarettes, and food and even activities such as exercise, watching TV, using electronic devices, working, and experiencing sensory highs. This precept concerns anything we can use to turn ourselves away from the immediate experience of our minds and bodies. So, in exploring this precept, we do not focus so much on what particular drugs or activities are legally or socially *acceptable* to use, but instead we examine our intentions. For one person or another, nearly any substance or activity can serve to drive them further into their habitual ways of meeting the events and circumstances of everyday life. My point is that alcohol, drugs, and TV—or whatever it might be for you—are not escapes in and of themselves. What makes them escapes is how we use them.

EVER CHANGING, EVER CLOUDING

What becomes clear after we've observed ourselves in action around this precept is that the clarity of which our minds are capable inevitably gets clouded over when we hand over our minds to compulsive consumption. Indeed, it's quite natural. It's the human condition. We may be able to cease the clouding caused by imbibing certain substances and engaging in certain activities, but the clouding of the mind is inevitable as we go about our lives as thinking, physical beings. Even people who rarely imbibe mind-altering substances or engage in activities known to cloud perception find they can learn from this precept. We need to think in order to get from one side of a room to another to answer the doorbell, or to turn the pages of this book. So, in a certain sense, we become intoxicated every time we have a thought. Being that we need to think as functioning human beings, we are therefore often intoxicated. When we consume substances or engage in activities to alter our experience, we just add literal intoxication to the "drunkenness" of our usual thinking!

As well, our brains are drug factories that send thousands of chemicals coursing through our body to regulate our moods and behaviors. Drugs that we consume voluntarily generally have their effect by virtue of their similarity to neurotransmitters, the natural chemical messengers that travel back and forth between neurons throughout your nervous system, carrying messages between the brain and the rest of the body. Melatonin produced in a daily rhythm induces sleep. Adrenaline, produced in response to danger, causes blood to be diverted to muscles in preparation for action, resulting in an extreme level of alertness. Endorphins are typically released in high dosages when we're in some kind of pain and are well known for causing what's called "runner's high." Serotonin release is associated with mood and has been used in synthetic form for decades in the treatment of depression. These substances occur naturally but can also be manipulated by drugs, exercise, food, and, indeed, many activities we engage in.

So what are we to do? The teaching of this precept, as with all the precepts, is to cultivate the clarity that keeps us alert and present so that we more quickly catch our swings into the habitual patterns of our reactions. The value of working with this precept is not to try to clear the clouds away forever but to come to understand that neither the clouds nor a clear mind alone is the fullness of life. Both arise and fall away as part of being human. Our intention is to know them as best we can and to not be attached to one or the other. Through our practice, we can have opening experiences wherein all thinking and the dream of self fall away completely. But the phone will ring, the kids will need to be picked up at school, bills will need to be paid, more dirty dishes will appear in the sink, and we'll have our reactions to all of these occurrences—and the clouds will reappear. The real question is, do we catch them before we swing into action?

I have found that the range of experiences of people working with this precept is very wide. Some people never drink or use drugs at all, and so they are convinced at the beginning that they could probably just skip over this one. Others have a history of substance abuse and are scared to death of facing this precept. Some people, in exploring this precept, find that they are dealing with a much deeper physical addiction than they had realized, and the sign above the door directs their way into treatment and recovery. Others come to it after years of recovery and want to explore the deeper patterns of their addictive behavior.

A good way to begin exploring this precept is to pick one substance or activity that you regularly engage in with some attachment (in other words, you'd have some reaction if you couldn't do it) and begin observing yourself internally while using or engaging in that activity. After you've practiced this way for a while and have a sense of what it feels like before, during, and after you have engaged in your preferred method of clouding, you can begin to inquire a little deeper by experimenting with extending your awareness. Take note of the thoughts and bodily sensations that arise before, doing, and after the action. For example, you may begin to notice that you often reach for the refrigerator door when you're bored or worried. Perhaps a jitteriness or depression might accompany a reach for the chocolate bar. Maybe your cell phone beckons you to get lost in a video game. These days, we have multiple ways, beyond drugs and drink, to cloud our awareness. When you're engaging in the action, what's the mind/body experiencing? What about immediately after?

STUDENT SHARING

Student: It strikes me how much we're steeped in a culture that constantly sends out messages that some mind or body experiences are okay while others are not. For example, it's okay to be on the go and active with unlimited energy, but not okay to get tired. I'm thinking about simple things like energy bars or energy drinks that we consume throughout the day to keep on going. It's like the message is: peak experience is the best experience, that there's something wrong if we want to slow down because we're tired. I sometimes wonder how all of this is tied into the larger value system of our culture, which seems to center on more is better.

Diane: It's no surprise that what we put into our bodies reflects what's in our heads. Maybe it is a reflection of our society. It's interesting to think about this, but we need to look to our own intention. The real practice comes in how we handle body or mind states we're not satisfied with—that don't meet the requirements we have come to rely on in order to avoid more core beliefs about who we think we are. If I have a deadline to meet, and I'm clean out of energy, I'll no doubt reach for a piece of chocolate or a cup of coffee. Remember, it's not the substance we're using that's key here; it's our intention in using it and the harm and suffering it causes when we use it to cloud our ability to take clear, intelligent action.

Student: As I work with this precept I realize that I have expectations that I *should* experience certain feelings around certain experiences. For example, I *should* feel happy when I get home from work at night and see my partner and kids. When I don't, I often reach for a beer or glass of wine so that I can relax and loosen up in order to enjoy them more. I know my intention is to relax, but would that be such a bad thing to do if it allows me to be there and enjoy my family more? Would you call this an addiction?

Diane: But are you really there? Would there be another way to be there and honor the tenseness, rather than ignoring it? This is what your practice can offer you. There are a lot of ways to talk about addiction. There is a physical addiction at a cellular level in which the organism comes to crave substances.

This is the level of addiction of the drug addict or alcoholic. Then there's a more general way of talking about addiction, much like what you might be describing here. I think of addiction in this way as a requirement that causes us to act in body, speech, and mind in a certain way so as to alter our experience. What is your requirement here?

Student: That I always be relaxed and enjoy coming home and being with my family.

Diane: And is that true? Are you always relaxed, and do you always enjoy being with your family when you come home?

Student: No.

Diane: Where is it written that you must always be relaxed and enjoy your family? This question is your point of entry. You've observed yourself in action, now you circle into the next spiral. Grab this question with your life—before you reach for the bottle of beer. You'll learn something. I don't know what that will be. This is your discovery. Own it. Your addiction is to your requirement—not the beer or wine.

I Take Up the Way of Taking Only What Is Freely Given and Giving Freely of All That I Can

This precept reflects back to the previous chapter's discussion of the Paramita of Giving and Receiving. It encourages us to consider deeply what we think we need and what is being offered to us directly. With this precept, we explore our beliefs about what we think we don't have, what we think we should have, and what we have. Sometimes this precept is worded as a prohibition against stealing, but its core goes deeper than just taking what is not ours to take. It invites us to consider deeply how we ask or don't ask for whatever it is we want or need. It invites us to consider how we offer or don't offer what we are capable of giving. It then leads us into a deeper examination of our notions of lacking and deserving—implicit beliefs that we require and deserve to have more than what we have.

At a subtler level, this precept directs us to the mind of "getting something." It encourages us to meet the beliefs, assumptions, and habitual thought patterns behind that door that fuel our drive and insistence on getting what we want. It leads us to uncovering the mind of attainment. And quite often, what fuels this need for attainment is the belief of not-enoughness, insufficiency, lack. The form this belief takes is different for all of us. It may be fueled by a sense of entitlement—being owed more than what you're receiving. It may be fueled by the belief that life will not support you, is not enough—that you are incomplete, vulnerable, small, and powerless. This precept offers us the opportunity to meet the world—our partners, our neighbors and friends, our children, and ourselves—beyond these patterns of thinking, recognizing the generosity, gratitude, and fullness of life even in the most ordinary of our daily activities.

PRACTICE

Begin to notice the obvious and subtle ways in which you take what is not yours to take or ways in which you hold back from giving freely all that you can. Include not just material items but also time, attention, and so forth. You may notice only obvious things in the beginning—it can take a while to catch some of the subtleties.

One of the difficulties in this first part of the exploration is that it's not always so clear as to what is freely being offered to you or by you. It's pretty clear if a cashier at the grocery store makes a mistake in your favor and you don't tell her or when you take company time to do personal business. It's also clear when you ignore a person on the street in obvious need of your help or when you don't meet your financial responsibilities when you have the resources to do so. But as we go about our life, it takes a little more intention to watch, look, and listen.

At work, notice how long you take for lunch, coffee, or bathroom breaks. At home, notice what you might indirectly take from your roommate, partner, or kids, such as time or attention. We can steal life's teachers from our children or loved ones under the guise of trying to protect them. It takes courage to give those teachings over to them.

In order to begin the process of observing your everyday actions at a closer magnification, choose one or two specific actions and get to know them better. Put them under your careful observation.

STUDENT SHARING

One of my students shared the following:

> After I had been observing my trip to work each day for a while, I realized that a sense of urgency continued as I competed for a parking spot, wormed my way into first place on the elevator, and tried to beat others to the coffee machine. I began to understand that the urgency, which I experienced as a tingling rush in my chest accompanied by short quick breathing, had something to do with thoughts such as, "If I don't get it then . . ." "Then what?" That question began to take hold. What did I think would be the worst thing that could happen if I didn't get that space in front of the car next to me? What is the worst thing that could happen

if I wasn't first on the elevator? Of course, I could answer these questions logically and would see that nothing very dreadful would happen, but nevertheless the concern was compelling me into a sense of urgency that propelled me into a sort of tunnel vision in which all I was aware of was what I thought I needed. Once more, the longer I stayed with the experience of feeling the need to take, the less I could find something I really needed to be urgent about.

What this student describes as *tunnel vision* is an important point because this is exactly what practice with this precept can reveal to us—the difference between *wanting* and *needing*. For example, we might say, I *need* you to give me a space in line, when what we really mean is I *want* you to give me a space in line. Sometimes we need; sometimes we just want or would like. Let's not confuse the two. Each has its place under specific conditions. When we know the difference, then we are free to take and free to give. But when not used in ways that fit the situation, can my unnecessary need actually limit another's legitimate need, limiting their option to say *no* or *yes* or *maybe*?

Talking about need versus want should not be spoken glibly here. This is an important point and one that we should all consider as we face the rising numbers of homeless families both in the US and around the world. Swollen bellies and wounds of exposure scream out loud and clear—*lack* and *need*. I'd steal a loaf of bread in a wink, if I had no money and I knew it would ward off starvation for myself or my children. But what we're talking about here is a different hunger. It is not a need arising out of basic survival. It is the mind of lacking that gives rise to envy, desire, greed, and a closed heart.

To practice giving freely of all that you can does not mean to empty your house of all its belongings. It doesn't even mean that you have to swing open your heart, letting go of all your defenses at once. It means to first come to know your resistance to giving and then to give what you can within that moment. Then, every day, just do one thing that goes against that pattern of holding back and see what your experience is when you open in that way.

I Take Up the Way of Engaging in Intimacy Respectfully and with an Open Heart

This precept offers the opportunity to become truly intimate —but that intimacy begins with ourselves, not others. It encourages us to face squarely how we may be using sexual intimacy as a way to avoid a deeper intimacy with our deepest longings and fears. Anytime we use sexual energy to escape or alter our present state of mind, we are also enclosing ourselves in a tighter circle of separation. Sexual energy is among the most potent of all human feelings. Its force and vigor arise from a host of potent biochemical factors, which can frighten us away or seduce us into addiction. Engaging in this precept reveals our beliefs about this potent energy and our consequent habits in how we hold it. Fragility, hostility, impotency, contempt, power, and safety are but a few of the ideas that can be bound up in our perceptions of sexual intimacy. When we allow these beliefs to enter into and cloud our understanding of intimacy, to get in the way of an open experience of sexuality as a pure, strong connection with others, we have not engaged with an open heart.

PRACTICE

Becoming aware of sexual energy. We begin our practice with this precept by purposefully bringing awareness to the physical sensations associated with sexual energy. A good place to begin practice with this precept is in the body—to explore some of the embodied beliefs and sensations that arise for us around sexuality. Taking your favorite comfortable position, bring your attention to the body. Stay relaxed, with a gentle focus on breathing in and out. Now bring into mind any image, sense, or word that excites you sexually. It can be a person, a picture, a smell, or a melody. It can be a word or phrase. If you notice yourself beginning to judge the object of your attention as good, bad, sick, or something else, just identify those thoughts as "judging" and return to the object of your attention. When you've activated something, you'll notice a change in your bodily experience. The breath may quicken, deepen, or shorten. The body may slightly contract or tighten. You may feel certain sensations. Or you may feel nothing. Feeling nothing is also an experience. What is that numbness like? Deepen the body awareness by paying closer attention to the heart, gut, and genital areas. Do some areas feel more remote than others? In other words, do you find that awareness doesn't go to certain areas? If it doesn't, try moving your attention in that direction and see what happens. Do any thoughts, emotions, or judgments, such as "I can't do this" or "I'm not good at this" arise around this numbness? If you notice feelings such as fear, shame, hurt, anger, or power, subvocalize the label and return to just breathing and feeling the sensation.

Remember, as in all inquiry, you're not demanding or measuring. You are just inviting by purposely bringing awareness to your point of inquiry. The power of this exercise is in the posing of questions that seek no answer. Don't necessarily expect your experience to be pleasurable or even sexual. The aim of this exercise is to bring into awareness what thoughts/beliefs you associate with sexual energy.

Sexual energy may rise—but fear, anger, shame, or other emotions may rise instead of it or piggyback on it.

Expanding the inquiry. Bring your inquiry into your daily experiences, noticing what sorts of reactions different situations bring up for you. Here, you are trying to bring out into the open not only your personal experience with sexual energy but also attitudes and judgments you may hold toward others regarding their sexuality. The intention at this point is to be as observant as possible of what goes on inside you on the street, in the bus, at work, or wherever you see or interact with others. Do certain types of people turn you off or on? Do you find yourself judging and closing yourself off from certain individuals? Give yourself permission to feel and think, unrestricted. Be open and observe whatever thoughts or feelings arise. Do you notice any patterns? As in the exercise above, keep your inquiry at the level of invitation. You are not demanding that anything reveal itself. You are simply removing veils that may be covering a more earnest experience of your sexuality.

You may do this exercise for days, weeks, or even months before you notice anything consciously. But if you are gentle and patient with yourself, over time, you will begin to open the door and find your deepest associations with sexual energy—how you experience it yourself and how you view it in others. Once you are able to do this, you can really begin to do the additional work of exploring the ways in which you may be using this energy to reinforce patterns of self-identity that can cloud *what is*.

We might think of our relationship to sex as somewhere between two bookends. On the one end is the engagement in pure wondrous sexual energy and communion—nothing to grasp, nothing to attach to. On the other extreme, sex can lead to clinging, alienation, and destructiveness.

I Take Up the Way of Letting Go of Anger

This precept helps us wake up to our particular relationship to anger, whether confronted in ourselves or in others. The key is to learn how to be awake in the presence of anger instead of swinging blindly into action. Practicing this precept reveals how anger can either dupe us into chasing shadows or inform us about situations and conditions that call for response. Perhaps especially for Buddhists, it is common to think that the experience or expression of anger is inappropriate, or a sign of an immature practice. The intention of this precept, however, is not to squelch all anger but rather to help us uncover deeply held beliefs about anger. By learning how to listen openly to the experience, seeing the tumultuous storm of thoughts and sensations settle, we find that we can be silent and still in the eye of the storm. And it is there that our deepest holdings are revealed. We see them clearly for what they are, and we take action out of that clarity. For some, it is held in the belief that it is wrong to be angry in any situation. For others, anger is worn like an armband that signals to others, "Don't mess with me." For some, anger is like a land mine waiting to be tripped by any unfortunate passerby, while for others, it supplies a sense of power and strength. And for many, anger remains mostly hidden, for it frightens its bearer into a secret silence. After working with this precept for some time, one of my students expressed it this way: "Anger no longer seems a lunatic stranger locked in the basement but a familiar shadowy twin who suddenly appears in the room in unexpected guises. I now recognize anger as a frequent visitor in my life."

Anger is a tricky emotion for many of us. It can seem to rise out of a stack of dirty dishes our housemate leaves in the sink, the homework our kids forgot to complete, or a piece of news concerning politics or culture. It can be directed outward, inward, or have no direction at all. It can be simmering, boiling over, felt, or disregarded. Its faces are many, and its force can strengthen or destroy. Its mask of power covers fear and powerlessness. It seems to have a power of its own appearing as little moments of madness, when reason and logic fall away. We may try to avoid it, ignore it, or hang on to it. We may identify it as "yours" or "mine."

STUDENT SHARING

Student: I understand what you are saying about remaining open and present to whatever the experience is, but sometimes I get so angry at my kids, I scare myself. I don't feel like I have an inch of space to experience in the middle of that heat. How would I practice with that?

Diane: Sometimes the heat of the anger is so intense that the lighthouse signals us not to look and listen but to just STOP. As a child, I was prone to mouthing off. My father would often tell me to zipper my mouth and count to ten. Counting to ten can be an excellent practice in the heat of rage. Breathe in, count one. Breathe out, count two. When the mind starts to go with the thinking, wrestle it back to one, two, three . . . Sometimes removing yourself from the situation by going for a walk or a run, locking yourself in the bathroom, or taking a cool shower or a long hot bath is the most skillful action to take in the heat of rage. Try listening to your favorite music. Try dancing. Equally as important as the practice of openly experiencing and inquiring into the habitual patterns of our behavior is to know when the heat gets too hot and we need out. There are times when the action that most serves life is to not take tea by the fire but to get out of the kitchen. A screaming child or two on a morning after a sleepless night can be a good time to quickly get some help with the situation.

Student: I'm thinking of the recent violence in the news spurred by the anger and hatred of one group for another. It can take the form of street gangs, a small group of kids in high school opening fire on another group, or something as big as terrorist groups. How is the anger I might feel toward my boss or my neighbor or my kids different from this type of group anger?

Diane: Anger is anger. There's no two ways about it. For sure, if you slap your child out of anger or you curse your neighbor or boss, that is, in a sense, different in outcome from, say, opening fire in a library filled with high school students or flying an airplane into a building. But in terms of anger, there's no difference. The difference is what we do with it.

Today we see a great deal of group hatred that takes the form of religious, ethnic, political, and ideological differences. What draws people together to take group action out of anger is each individual person's anger within that group. The group may serve as a container for the individual's anger, but it does not create it. That comes from the individual. So when we witness some of the atrocities in the world that we have of late, it seems to me that we are witnessing, in part, what happens when an individual's fear, hopelessness, powerlessness, and so forth get recognition within a larger group. The individual's reactions to those experiences are generalized and legitimized, at least within the group, and any hope of self-inquiry is lost.

If we were always free of our dream of who we think we are, there would be no anger, no need for a precept. But one way or another we do have moments of anger, unless we're completely free of all our self-centered thinking. Intelligent practice remembers that the value of practicing with the precepts lies not in how it measures our distance along the idealized path to enlightenment but rather how it helps us live in the everyday circumstances of our life. In the real life most of us live, we yell at our kids, we shout back at our partner, we get angry with our political leaders, and so forth.

So rather than trying not to become angry, the most helpful way of working with the precept is to watch what happens when anger arises. In the open listening of the experience, the tumultuous storm of thoughts and sensations calms as we open and allow our awareness to settle into the eye of the storm. What is revealed there are our holdings, our stubborn insistence that life follow our agenda. We see them clearly for what they are, and we take action out of that open clarity.

I Take Up the Way of Supporting Life

Quite often, this precept is taken as a vow to not take life. While this is certainly an integral part of it, it is even more an affirmation to support life. It takes a lot more courage and often sacrifice to put into action our aspirations to support life than to kill it. Understood in this way, taking up the way of supporting life is not an injunction to never kill but rather a directive to become more aware of the unquestionable life force in all things and how we intentionally or unintentionally ignore or interrupt it.

Robert Oppenheimer, the physicist who directed the Manhattan Project, which produced the first nuclear bombs, is said to have been walking in the woods one day with a friend, in the years after the war had ended. He came across a land turtle and, thinking it would make a nice surprise for his grandson back at the house, picked it up to carry it home. But just a few meters along the path, he stopped abruptly, turned back, and placed the turtle on the ground precisely where he had picked it up. He remarked to his friend, "I have interfered with life enough for one man's lifetime."

What strikes me about Oppenheimer's insight is not only what seems to be a recognition of his part in the creation of the first nuclear bomb and weapon of mass destruction, but also the subtler, often unrecognized way in which our most ordinary, sometimes well-intentioned actions, such as bringing a land turtle as a gift to a grandchild, can be an action that does not support life. While we all, at times, will likely face larger questions of taking life, such as whether or not to take up arms in war, euthanasia (be it for another human or a family pet), abortion, death penalty, etc., the subtler ways in which this precept interweaves into our daily living are less obvious and require cultivating keen awareness of life itself. Over time, what we come to realize is that to live means to take life and to take life means to live. Every time we drink water to hydrate our body, we kill millions of microorganisms. Every time we take a refreshing walk across the sweet green grass in the park, we kill innumerable tiny creatures. We cannot escape taking life so that we can survive, and, at the same time, we can support life in whatever way we can.

If we aspire to live in ways that support life, then first we must open the door when the killer in us knocks. Working with this precept openly can eventually reveal some aspects of ourselves we would rather keep hidden. Recently, several people shared with me the agony of caring for aging parents with dementia. Worn down by endless calls and emergencies, hardly being able to keep up with life's ordinary challenges of work and family, these people opened their hearts to themselves by acknowledging that there are indeed times when they hope that the next call would inform them that their parent has died—"There are times, when I just want him to die! I want to be free of this responsibility!" This is when we take refuge in the precept, for it encourages us to listen. As with the anger precept, the precept of supporting life directs us toward breathing in the presence of just this. Just this heat or hurt—or whatever is the experience of your life in this moment.

But to support life, we must first be aware of all the less obvious, subtle, seen and unseen life around us. We begin our work with this precept by cultivating an intention to bring awareness of life around us. In our busy world, much of the time, we miss the most obvious life forces in our surroundings like blades of grass poking through cracked cement on the sidewalk or a waft of microorganisms in the damp earth or sewer rising from the ground after a rainstorm. To support life, we need to engage with life, and to engage with life, we need to first be awake to its subtleties. And we cannot become aware without engaging effort. We need to put down our phone, unplug our ears, look down, look up, look right, left, and forward. We need to pay attention! Right now, as you hold this book in your hands, can you say what phase the moon is in? When last did you really look up at the night sky?

PRACTICE

Every morning when you wake up and every night before you go to bed, turn your head to the sky. Fully take it in, letting your vision fully receive. Is it dead or alive?

For at least twenty minutes every day, unhook yourself from your electronic devices, sit down, and take in your complete surroundings, watching for all signs of life. Perhaps a fly buzzes your nose, an ant crawls along the table, a half-eaten apple dries on the table. If you're outside, look around at the trees, the buildings, the people in the street. See what life comes into your field of vision. Say quietly to yourself: "You are life; I am life; we are life."

Extend the above foci to include more and more of your waking hours. In time, you may find that it's impossible to find a place without life.

Begin to notice what offers its life to support your life. This awareness can range from eating a hamburger to drinking a glass of water. Again, over time your awareness will grow and with it your appreciation for all of life.

Consider the ways in which you support life. Try to keep it simple and ordinary.

STUDENT SHARING

Student: One of the things I noticed practicing with this precept is how easy it is for me to take care to recycle my plastics, paper, and so forth and to participate in any of the other numerous ecological practices for supporting the life of the planet, and yet when it comes to just being awake to the life of the planet itself, I'm a bit numb. This practice you describe has been hard for me mostly because I find I'm addicted a bit to spacing out, or, I might say, leaving out, much of life that's presenting itself each and every moment. I'm saddened by this and a bit embarrassed that I've been thinking I'm so "with it" when I'm really "not with it."

Diane: And now, in this realization, are you with it or not with it? This is the practice for all of us—bring up the intention, put forth the effort, receive, and give. Life takes care of the rest.

Student: What's interesting for me is that I notice when I bring the intention to give my attention to whatever comes my way, I actually connect with others more easily. Yesterday, as I was walking to my bus stop, instead of looking at my phone, I put it in my pocket and looked at the sidewalk and street gutter. I didn't see any grass or weeds poking up, but I did see a shoe, a foot, a leg of a person leaning against a building. For a moment, I really connected with the realization that this is a living, thriving person. Before he became a street person in my mind, he was simply an expression of the life force. I was deeply moved, and it lasted just a moment.

Diane: And this is taking up the way of supporting life.

4

Practicing Patience

KSHANTI PARAMITA

If this present moment is lived whole-heartedly
and meticulously, the future will take care of itself.
—Alan Arkin, *An Improvised Life*

WE'VE ALL heard it before, these directives that suggest we
could get off, or at least pause from, whatever trajectory our
habits have set us on. But it's not always so easy. There are
many reasons why we want to plow through our day-to-day
encounters, ignoring or denying the fact that life's events are
not on our terms. And we risk missing the precious unfolding
of life as it is right now in the pursuit of an imagined future
outcome or destination. What the Paramita of Practicing
Patience encourages us to do is to explore more deeply what
it means to rest in and fully engage in the truth of each moment. It encourages us to explore what drives us away from
experiencing the reality of the present and instead ushers us
into an imagined projection of something different. What is our
experience as we sit in our car in the snail's pace of rush hour
traffic, or as we watch the clock when the doctor is running an
hour behind our scheduled appointment? Where is our mind

when we listen for the umpteenth time to the same story from our elderly uncle or grow dispirited, angry, or resentful when, in spite of the efforts of many well-intended people, political leaders around the world continue to ignore the well-being of people and the planet?

STUDENT SHARING

One of my students shared the following account:

It was a busy day in the small, crowded copy shop, and I had just a few minutes to have some important documents copied before the next mail pickup. I could see that the two young women behind the counter were somewhat flustered trying to keep up, and I made a small note to myself to be what we commonly call "patient." In other words, just wait. My turn at the counter came, and, as quickly as one in and out breath, I swept aside the actual situation in the shop—the number of people asking for help, the overloaded workers, the frenzied energy. I blocked all that out and zoned in on what I needed done. As I described to the young woman the way I wanted the copying done, within a short period of time I realized that she completely misunderstood what I was saying and was in fact taking my comment as a criticism or accusation of sorts. She lashed out that I was asking her to make a copy of something in a way that she wasn't permitted to do. When I began to question her, she became more upset, and it wasn't long before we both stepped out of the reality of the situation before us and into our personal domains of self-righteous anger.

Mine, of course, was subtler, skillfully delivered in my "Zen student" voice. But inside, I was furious! So, I left the shop. I even had thoughts of reporting her "unprofessional" behavior to whomever her boss happened to be. But I had only walked about thirty feet out of the door when a voice deep inside came forward and said, "Yes, you're really angry, but hold off. Don't do anything yet. Wait. Pay attention." This was the first utterance of the Paramita of Practicing Patience: "Be where you are." So, I paused for a few moments and felt the anger and disappointment at myself for letting my emotions get out of hand. I was angry with her for steadfastly accusing me of something I didn't do, and, in truth, for stepping out of her role of "the customer is always right." In short, "How dare her!" was utmost in mind. And in the midst of it all, I began to hear the rising sensations of guilt and the old voices of "should" and "should not." But again, the whispered voice of Practicing Patience counseled, "Let in. Don't block out. Lean into the parameters of the circle and let it widen." So, over the next few days, I engaged in Practicing Patience.

And it began with bearing witness to the anger and righteousness that loomed foremost in my thoughts. It began with bearing witness to my own experience and then bearing witness to the other person. Even though it was in the past, the woman's face came forward, and I saw the tears in her eyes and heard the quiver in her voice—both of which I had blocked out in the heat of anger. Then "openness and possibility" arose and fell away in waves. The circle of awareness widened to include possibilities of the situation she might be facing that were unknown to me.

After several days of this practice, right action came forth. Not out of some external set of guidelines or rules of right action but rather from the deep-marrow knowing that the right thing to do was to apologize. So, early the next morning, before the lines of people demanding copies began to form, I went to the copy store. Luckily, just outside the shop, I met the

young woman with whom I had had the encounter. I reminded
her of who I was and said, "I am sorry for what took place the
other day and apologize if my words were hurtful." At first,
she didn't remember, but when I described the situation, she
immediately reacted defensively, saying that I accused her of
something she wasn't guilty of. This time, I heard her. I don't
know why she felt the need to cling to that story. The point is,
that was what she was doing. That was the way it was going
to be, no matter how much I tried to explain my point of view
in those few moments. And in bearing witness to her view of
the situation, I could hold it, even though I didn't agree with
it. In that moment of practicing patience, I found words I
could speak from the heart and simply said, "I understand you
feel that way, and I am sorry if my words upset or hurt you.
I truly wish you no harm and wish you well." She was silent
for a moment and then she smiled a bit. She left perhaps still
believing her story.

Elements of Practicing Patience

Practicing Patience is often described as tolerance or forbearance. The word *tolerance*, meaning "endurance" and
"fortitude," implies nonjudgmental acceptance. Sometimes
Practicing Patience is mistakenly thought to have something
to do to with resignation, putting up with things we don't
agree with. But this paramita asks for more than a mental
shrug of the shoulders. Tolerance is action, not inaction. If
we're tolerant of others' points of view, it doesn't mean we
don't take action.

Practicing Patience is also acknowledging that we are human and can easily get caught up in intolerance or impatience. It is a humble recognition that we are capable of doing great good and great harm. So, being patient with our impatience is also included in this paramita. And most of us live our life straddling a line down the middle. Forbearance implies a strength, a sense of "steady as you go." It implies being solid, having both feet on the ground. Not to be confused with rigidity, forbearance is something that can be depended on. We live in relationship, but relationship implies more than us alone. Over time, and through a recognition of relationship, we find that we and other are one. And, of course, most of us don't believe this for a moment. So this is where the practice of tolerance and forbearance supports us. It's not always easy, for sure, but it's an absolute necessity.

Practicing Patience also brings up forgiveness. I think of forgiveness as letting go of the past. It's the "letting go" part that's most important. And just as tolerance doesn't mean inaction, forgiveness doesn't mean we deny or even perhaps forget hurtful actions. Rather it means we let go of harboring resentment and wanting some sort of retaliation. Resentment is really interesting because we can be surprised at how it hides in the dark corners of our experience. If our mind is focused only on what this person did to us in the past, it's very unlikely we're going to meet them fully in the present. And unless we meet people and situations in the present, there's little hope for patience.

But Practicing Patience is even more than this, for it leans us into what prevents us from allowing, from being open. It offers freedom from control. It challenges us to turn toward the total presence and freedom of just this.

STUDENT SHARING

One of my students shared the following account:

While driving home one night from downtown Oakland, a bit tired and anxious to get home, I noticed that the car in front of me came to an abrupt halt. There was no traffic light, and from my perspective, no apparent reason for stopping. My thoughts and body snapped into frustration and rising anger. Tightening my fingers on the wheel, gritting my teeth a bit, I started to have thoughts like, "What are you stopping for? Don't you know how to drive?" Anger had hijacked my being present. All my body and mind knew was that I was tired, and I wanted to get home, and the driver in front of me was slowing me down. I was squeezed into the tiny closed circle of me—what I want, what I think I need; in short, a little self-centered view of the situation. Then suddenly, a pedestrian crossed in front of the car in front of me. I realized that I was so caught up in my own impatience to get home, I completely left out of my awareness any other possibilities as to why that car had stopped. I remember feeling like a splash of cold water had hit my face: "Hey, wake up. It's not always about you!" Patience is what we have with the people driving the cars behind us, and impatience is what we have with the people driving the cars in front of us.

There's Always More Than Meets the Eye

As the above story illustrates, when we for just a few moments remember that we may not be seeing the whole picture, we enter into Practicing Patience. And over time, we come to realize that we never know the whole situation. We can only do our best, and that is enough. This alone is a great antidote to impatience. All is not as it appears. In any situation, there's us and much more than us, as it was with this student's car experience. But opening our eyes, ears, and mind to what we unconsciously may be blocking out takes more than simple intention. We need to practice tuning our senses to be more receptive. This all-inclusive view is how Zen master Thich Nhat Hanh describes the Paramita of Practicing Patience: "When we practice inclusiveness, we don't have to suffer or forbear, even when we have to embrace suffering and injustice."[1]

PRACTICE

Choosing an impatient situation. Choose a simple situation in which you frequently find impatience arising. For example, it could be sitting at a traffic light or waiting for your computer to kick in, your morning tea water to boil, or the elevator to arrive. It's best to choose a situation that occurs most days. Keep in mind that the purpose of practicing any of the paramitas is not to strong-arm your way into accomplishing them but rather to lean into the barriers that keep that which is deep within from coming forth. So, each time you lean into impatience, you will probably have lots of thoughts and feelings—especially anger, which is often considered the energy that blocks Practicing Patience.

As you wait for the traffic light, or whatever you're practicing with, give yourself complete permission to bear witness to whatever arises. Remember, nothing you experience is your enemy unless you make it so. Are your teeth clenching? Is there a tightness in the body? If so, where? Note the thoughts. Do they have a theme? Allow your breath to bear the weight of your experience. The breath, which bridges us into and out of life, is profoundly capable of carrying whatever we experience. Give control over to it, breathing in and out, with the intention to remain open to your experience. You may find that you will need to intentionally do this practice for several days, weeks, months, or depending on the situation, for the rest of your life! But if you choose something small for this introductory practice, you should notice over time that it's easier to simply rest in the breath of the experience.

At this point, begin expanding your awareness by taking in more of your surroundings. Again, it's very important to keep it simple. For example, if you're sitting in your car, look through the window in front of you. Really take it in. What do you notice? Listen to the sounds around you. Really listen—openly. What do you notice? The hum of the engine? What about smell? What about the feel of the steering wheel in your hand? Again, take your time. There's no schedule. Give yourself the rest of your life! As you practice with this same situation over days, weeks, or months, begin expanding your awareness. What else do you notice about the situation you tend to feel impatient with? What are you leaving out?

Listening patiently. Listening to others speak can be a particularly powerful method for practicing patience. What I'm talking about here is not just what might be called "engaged listening" or a kind of listening whereby we give certain verbal and gestural signals like nodding and so forth. This is a kind of listening in which we are totally present and that in and of itself gives the message that we are totally listening. You can't fake it. Notice the thoughts that arise when you want to interrupt. What happens to your body stance? Your facial expression? Your breathing? Remember that your mouth can remain closed, but you may be screaming on the inside, so pay attention to your inner experience. Then bring your attention to the voice you're listening to. It may be in person or coming from the TV or the radio or elsewhere. Listen closely to the voice itself and allow the sound of the words to just enter your ears. Try to keep this as immediate as possible. It will probably be a very short time before the thought about the voice and words will interfere with just listening. If you can do it for just a minute or two, you may find that you hear things that broaden your awareness of the situation—insights that are blotted out immediately when we're focused on a retort.

Allowing Vulnerability with Open Questioning and Open Listening

> Be patient toward all that is unsolved in your heart and love the questions themselves as if they were locked rooms or books written in a very foreign language. Don't search for the answers, which could not be given to you now, because you would not be able to live them. And the point is to live everything. Live the questions now. Perhaps then, someday far in the future, you will gradually, without even noticing it, live your way into the answer.
> —Rainer Maria Rilke, *Letters to a Young Poet*

As this Rilke quote suggests, patience can be more than simply waiting for an anticipated outcome. Patience can be a process of inquiry that involves far more than waiting. An honest question is a question that comes from not knowing. It's not a challenge or a debate but rather a true inquiry that, even if only for a moment, originates beyond the boundaries of our safety zones. This open questioning takes courage because it asks us to stand alone, without our preconceived views of people and events. It invites a true sense of "I wonder." And because it's open, our view is forced to widen.

I think of open questioning as what happens when we send a space probe into dark space. When that probe is propelled into the unknown, we have no idea what information will come back to us, if any. And yet the power is in the asking, for it opens our minds to possibilities. Scientists know that the questions are as important as the answers, and it's questions that keep scientific inquiry alive and vital. But in spite of this truth, it seems we live in a world growing less tolerant of sustained questioning. We want quick answers and quick fixes, whether it's how to fix a broken appliance or how to make our relationship work better. I wonder what's happening to those precious "I wonder how or if . . ." moments that give us space to not only ponder and consider various options but also to exercise our problem-solving capacities. Not so long ago, when I had a question about how to go about fixing something in my home, I would research it perhaps by asking a neighbor or friend or going to a library to look for a book on the subject. Now, I just go on YouTube, and I have a choice of videos that show me how to do it. No need for me to talk to anyone or figure anything out. Is that a blessing or something else, perhaps a loss? In Zen teaching, don't-know mind is most precious.

Taking the Long View: The Way of Hope

> Who can by stillness, little by little
> make what is troubled grow clear?
> Who can by movement, little by little
> make what is still grow quick?
> —Ursula K. Le Guin, *Tao Te Ching*

Practicing patience can indeed be described as waiting, but it is a particular type of waiting, one that is an essential component of hope. Václav Havel, the dissident and former president of the Czech Republic, describes a type of waiting that is related to hopelessness. With this type of waiting, there is a sense of no way out, of powerlessness. The will to take individual or group action is lost, and at best there is false hope that someone or some event beyond individual action will remedy the situation. But, as Havel points out, this is "but an illusion and is the product of our own helplessness, a patch over a hole in the spirit. . . . It is the hope of people without hope."[2] He goes on, however, to describe a second type of waiting, which can also be defined as practicing patience. This type of waiting includes skillful action. As we learned in our discussion of the precepts, taking skillful action is doing the right thing, that which supports life. Yes, we may *hope* it does good, but we are not attached to that outcome. We do it because it's the right action, and we turn from speculating whether our action will lead to a specific outcome today, tomorrow, or ever. The strength of Practicing Patience rests in taking action because it is the right thing to do, not because it assures a particular outcome. This is deep hope.

PRACTICE

There are three steps to engaging Practicing Patience.

1. Begin with yourself. Become familiar with your personal body stance when you feel frustrated or "antsy" or sense any signal that you are experiencing what is commonly called "impatience." Do you hold your breath? Do your shoulders tighten? Everyone's body has its unique repertoire of ways to express impatience. Become curious about yours. Notice how you meet these signals. Do thoughts of blame, denial, or impatience with the impatience arise? Is there any emotional tone? If so, just

note the emotion/thought and turn your effort toward bearing witness to physical sensations, just resting in the experience. You are now practicing patience with impatience. Bearing witness to ourselves in this way is what my teacher, Joko Beck, described as "suffering intelligently."

2. Expand your view to include what you're leaving out of the situation. Without turning away from whatever you've been experiencing in the first step, turn your effort to a more expanded view by simply asking, "What am I leaving out?" You can also think of this step as turning your energy toward leaning into the circumference of your circle so that it expands.

3. Accept where you are. With steps one and two, you have given witness to the truth of your experience. In doing so, you have stayed connected to the experience of whatever you are engaged with, and being just this moment is the way of compassion.

Sometimes it seems that this paramita is one of the hardest of all the paramitas to practice, for it asks us to persevere in the midst of great difficulty. But Practicing Patience is more than simply enduring or getting through difficult times. It asks us to take refuge in just continually knowing that no matter how things turn out, we will engage fully in life's circumstances. So Practicing Patience asks us to cultivate determination and engage effort, which is, as it turns out, our next paramita.

5

Engaging Effort

VIRYA PARAMITA

Go straight on a narrow road with 99 curves.
—Zen koan

Wholehearted Effort

The fourth paramita asks us to explore the difference between *doing* and *engaging*. It invites us to engage our capacity for perseverance, determination, and wholeheartedness in whatever life sends our way. It is fueled by our intention to engage with our life and the world in a way that is beneficial and supports life. We may feel helpless and hopeless, but if we hold to our vow to help others, the Paramita of Engaging Effort will support us in continuing forward.

Even so, a distinction about effort needs to be made. Oftentimes our effort is fueled by the belief that if we just push hard enough and make the "right" effort, we can create the life we want. This approach is not surprising given that we are flooded with messages from our consumer-driven culture that we can purchase anything—not just with money but also with our energy and attention: Eat this superfood and buy these vitamins for health and well-being. Buy this book that will change your life. Follow this teacher who will give you the secret to peace. Meditate with this special method. This is not to say that there are not certain things that can be of help to us, but, inevitably, there are times when our best-laid plans and hardest efforts fail to bring us what or to where we intended. To agree that life's road is windy and sometimes narrow is easy. But to walk that narrow windy road with its ninety-nine turns takes a particular type of effort. No matter what we engage in, it always comes down to just putting one foot in front of the other, for wholehearted effort is wholehearted action.

Zen master Dainin Katagiri Roshi reminds us that when we want to cross a river, we begin by taking one step forward. The idea, of course, is that we will continue taking steps; we may even decide to calculate the time and the number of steps needed to reach our goal. However, if we turn our full, wholehearted awareness toward the step itself, then one step becomes one hundred steps, and the distance between the two shores is contained within the earnest effort of that one step. In one step, we reach the other shore with wholehearted effort.[1]

The Chinese character used to translate *virya* means what we often refer to as "single-minded," "vigorous," or "strong." *Virya* also means "to move forward" or "keep trekking." Not to be confused with "pushing," virya is a "steady as you go" effort. When I watch a toddler's determination to climb up on something to reach a toy, I'm reminded of this kind of effort. I find it when I look into my friend's smiling face as she greets me from the hospital bed where she is receiving treatment for incurable cancer.

Wholehearted effort is about fully engaged living. It encourages us to question our beliefs about what we think our life *should be* and to turn our effort toward full presence of *how it is*. But even though this is simple, it's not always so easy. For one thing, being fully present means being fully present to everything, and that takes effort and perseverance. This is the first step—seeing and questioning, exploring and leaning into the expectation of *should* and allowing it to fall to the side for a moment. This, of course, is easier said than done and is not accomplished without intention, effort, and determination. When we hold on to our views, we try to exclude those aspects of our life that are really invitations for us to enter into the abundance of all that life is offering us. With wholehearted effort, it becomes possible to move again and again into that more abundant connection to our lives.

Clear Intention and Vow

Someone said to me recently, "The longer I practice, the more I realize the impossibility of keeping my vows." I responded, "Wonderful. Your vows are working. Hold to your vows." I've seen the word *vow* defined as "an engine that drives human aspiration, advancement, and accomplishment," and this is certainly the case, but the function of a vow is also to support us in a basic contradiction, which is that we can never fulfill our vows completely. This contradiction, however, is not an obstacle but rather a path, a gateway for us to meet life with an open heart and clear seeing. It is a path that, in the midst of our human imperfections, helps us return to our commitment to waking up and doing what we can to meet the suffering of the world with wise action. A vow is also what fuels

my young son and husband that we turn around and go back down the mountain. The trip was a huge success—although I didn't think so at the time. I hadn't made it to the top of the mountain, and I therefore thought I had failed. It was only in retrospect that I was able to appreciate that I did walk the narrow, climbing switchbacks of that beautiful country one foot, one breath at a time for many hours. With my thoughts on the destination, however, I missed the journey. The experience became a success in that it was also a step in my journey of learning to appreciate the present rather than fixating on the success or failure of attaining a goal.

When effort is put forth with our focus solely on the endgame—to win, to be successful, to get to the top of the mountain—then we miss the journey itself. Whereas effort done with the intention only to engage fully each step of the way—each deep breath, each wipe of sweat off the brow, and, yes, each doubt—"Why did I agree to this trip?"—knows no success or failure. Engaging in our life this way is to live for the joy of living. It is the path of hope.

Sometimes people will begin a meditation practice because they want to make their life fuller. More specifically, they may want to have less stress, achieve greater productivity, or change their personality. In and of itself, having goals such as these is not wrong. In fact, a goal can be the very thing that gets us to take that first step. But over time, the "newness" of the practice and the initial enthusiasm begin to settle. This is what is supposed to happen because, as we will see in the next chapter on the Paramita of Meditating, entering into quiet stillness over time is supposed to bring us face to face with who we *think* we are. This is a necessary but often difficult realization for the beginner practitioner. Engaging Effort is the practice that guides us along this windy, narrow road we call "our life."

Accepting Responsibility

Engaging Effort also requires accepting responsibility for and ownership of our lives. Are the fatigued parents who are woken in the middle of the night by a screaming, hungry baby always joyous about having their sleep disturbed? Why do they get up and feed the baby? Most simply, it's because it's their responsibility. To be a good parent doesn't mean one always makes the right choice and never a single mistake but rather that one has fundamentally accepted responsibility for one's children. Can we take this same approach in our jobs, with our neighbors, with the parts we play in world events?

In a certain sense, the baby screaming for a feeding is quite simple. The need is clear, and you meet it. The boss says, "Look, this project is due in two weeks, and you need to have it done." No options. You know you must get it done or you'll lose your job. No wiggle room, so you just do it. You don't have to want to do it. You might notice your feelings, your personal reactions to such situations, but they don't dictate the situation; you do it because it needs to be done. I am not speaking here of taking responsibility in the sense of being "the responsible person," the person who takes on the task even when it's not required. In this case, responsibility may well be serving our self-identity rather than whatever genuine need presents itself. What I'm getting at is a sense of responsibility as part of the effort to engage the present moment, the wholeheartedness that keeps us from succumbing to the trance of busyness. When you see a paper cup on the sidewalk on your way to work, whose responsibility is it to pick it up and deposit it in a trash container?

A Zen koan says, "Stop the sound of the distant temple bell." The usual focus of this koan is to present a way to stop a bell that, in our usual way of thinking, is far out of our reach. However, for the purposes of this discussion, I would like to focus on the hearing and listening of the bell itself. We cannot stop the sound of the bell unless we hear it, and we can't hear it unless we put forth the effort to train our ears to listen. In the same way, we cannot take wise action until we put forth the effort to listen carefully. The bells that call us to action come in all forms—a baby crying in the middle of the night, the alarm that wakes us up to get ready to go to work or to meditation, a suspicious lump under the arm. Bells, when heeded, set wheels into action. They summon us to gather energy and make effort—placing our feet on the cold floor, dialing the doctor's number to make an appointment. Sometimes, we just answer the alarm to wake up and get moving, and we don't necessarily know where we'll end up. It's an invitation that we choose to accept. And if this type of effort stems from wise action, then it is an essential element of deep hope.

There are many bells in the world ringing for us every second of the day. Some are ringing the sound of screaming babies as bombs fall on their rooftops. Some are ringing the sound of shivers as a man huddles into a corner of a building in our neighborhood, trying to escape the cold rain. Some are ringing the hate-filled shouts of extremists and so on. Do we hear those bells? Make no mistake, no matter how much we meditate, unless we are striving to open our ears and sound the bell wisely, we are not truly on the path.

Vigor and Perseverance

Engaging Effort has a vigorous momentum that continues, step by step, no matter how many detours and turns we find on our path. This is not a gym workout kind of vigor but rather a steady-as-you-go perseverance. Does it mean we always do it perfectly? Does it mean that we don't turn around and go down the mountain as I did on my first backpacking trip? The point is that wise effort just continues, one step at a time, taking life as the journey.

Courage in the Face of Vulnerability

Courage is another attribute of Engaging Effort, as it directs us toward facing the core fears and resistances that block us from receiving life's energy. Whenever there's something we'd just as soon turn away from, courageous energy says, "Look." When we allow ourselves to engage this energy, it brings us closer to what we believe makes us vulnerable. If we are experiencing a strong emotion, we might take on the practice of just experiencing the energy behind the thoughts about that emotion. When experiencing frustration or anger, we can use the Paramita of Engaging Effort to turn our attention from the accompanying thoughts—"It's his fault I feel this way," or "She's the one who caused this mess"—first toward the naming of the accompanying emotion and then toward the physical experience itself. We may notice that what we are calling "anger" is really a physical sensation residing somewhere in our body—a tenseness in the jaw, a tightening of the gut. And if, as we turn our awareness toward the sensation, we allow it to be present, we may experience it as an energy that feels hot, icy, jittery, or . . . Behind every emotion, there is a physical sensation, and by making the effort to turn our attention toward that sensation rather than avoiding it, we can come to know it wholeheartedly in a way that is open and free. No one else can do this for us. Engaging the situations and conditions of our lives, meeting our fears and resistances, keeping on with it, not turning back, and doing our very best—this is the Paramita of Engaging Effort.

STUDENT SHARING

Student: One of the things that I bump up against is a feeling of compulsion to be perfect. It's a sense of inadequacy masquerading as Engaging Effort. The thought is, "You should be doing more." It's characterized by a sense of anxiety or a sense of desperation rather than just that this is what needs to be done.

Diane: The point is not whether or not we take a certain action but to what percentage that action is done with wholehearted effort. Sometimes it'll be 5 percent wholehearted effort—effort without thought of gain. And other times it'll be 99 percent because we have given over completely: this is what we do. The point is to just bring awareness to the thoughts of "gain." Let them pass through and turn your attention to what's in front of you.

Student: I've come to realize I've lived much of my life so focused on trying to please others or be perfect that it didn't matter to me whether my energy level was high or low. It didn't matter, it didn't exist, and it wasn't anything I paid attention to. Since I began Zen practice, I can actually tell when I have high energy and when I have low energy. It's interesting because right now I'm in the seventh month of pregnancy, and I said the day before yesterday to my husband, "I can feel the life force at the moment being sucked out of me, and it's going into this baby," and I can see that difference. I can see and feel the difference, so it's just interesting to talk about energy because I don't think it's something that I had any real sense of for a long time until now. It just helps me to be able to put words to my experience.

Diane: You're bringing up a very important point. This paramita is in no way suggesting that we exhaust ourselves to do what needs to be done. Sometimes the wise action is to say, "I really can't take this other thing on. I've just got too much stuff on my plate." That's facing things as they are, meeting things as they are. In this way, we serve life, not our self-centered dream.

Student: I'm having trouble with discerning when I need to put forth effort in spite of being tired or whatever and when I'm ignoring the tired and doing it for some other reason. What's hard is when there's discernment involved, like is this what needs to be done or have I taken on too much? How do I discern what really needs to be done? There are times when it feels like physical energy isn't there, mental energy isn't there, it even seems like the heart energy isn't there, and I just feel like I'm going through the motions. I'm doing it because it's something I've started.

Diane: So is that different than what needs to be done? *Who* needs it to be done? That's one way to get inside that. Just add that little question. *Who* is it that needs it to be done? That'll bring you right inside what's driving this effort at a deeper level.

Student: I find transitions between one activity and another difficult. I can be concentrating on giving myself to whatever is in front of me, and then when that's done, that's where I get sort of lost. Where do I go from here? I've learned to ask myself, what do I need to do now? And things become clear, and the next thing to do just pops right up, but in that gap is where I have the trouble. It's like the commitment has to be remade and remade, but you have to be aware so as not to get sidetracked.

Diane: Rest in that gap between actions. Explore what happens in there without thinking so much about "I have to get on to the next thing." Sometimes it is the requirement to *do* that is what lures us away from where and for what we engage effort.

Student: Sometimes I feel I just don't want to make any effort. It's not that I'm tired or need rest, but it's more like an ennui, a lack of excitement. I'm not really depressed, but I find that I just procrastinate. Yet, five minutes later, if a friend calls to go out to a movie, or if something else catches my interest, I have all kinds of effort. My question is, what do I do in those times?

Diane: When we experience both energy and lack of energy with no apparent physical or psychological reason, we're likely to think that the times when we have energy to engage are preferable. And, of course they are, in a way. But in terms of meeting these situations as teachers, we would not favor one or the other.

PRACTICE

Becoming friends with your Engaging Effort behavior. Begin by noticing where or when you put forth less effort and pay attention to what your full experience is at such times. See if you can pick up what you're experiencing physically, emotionally, and mentally. Don't try to change it. Just become familiar with it and see if there are any patterns.

After sticking with the first step long enough to notice patterns, choose a certain kind of experience and decide to engage it more fully. Your decision to engage with lack of effort is effort itself. For example, oftentimes students will share with me that they are having trouble doing their meditation each day. I suggest the Engaging Effort practice of just making the promise each day to stand in front of their meditation place and count ten breaths. If they choose to carry through with the meditation, fine, but that is not the point. The point of this practice is to fan the deeper intent to practice, to give the ember of bodhicitta[2] a chance to glow.

Taking the first step. Another version of the above practice is to just take one action in the direction of what it is you want to do. Notice what comes up when you take that step. Listen to your body. Notice your thinking. Listen and decide whether or not to believe your thoughts or to just set them aside and move forward. I often use this practice when it's time for me to take my morning walk. I am not a great lover of exercise, but I do know it's essential that I get exercise every day. On the days I really don't want to make an effort, and there's no practical reason for me not to walk, I make a bargain with myself by saying, "I only need to walk to the front gate. At that point I can choose to come back into the house, or I can go farther." Ninety-nine percent of the time, I go farther, and I learn something.

No Hope without Engaging Effort

Zen master Dogen tells the story of a student who visits his master one cold day. Upon entering the room, the master asks the student to poke around in the fireplace to see if there are any embers still burning. The student pokes around and says, "Nope. It's dead." The master then stands up, goes to the fireplace with a poker, and, after searching around, finds a very small ember. Showing it to the student, he says, "Isn't this fire?" The student gets the message and thanks the master. The master goes on: "If we contemplate Buddha Nature, we realize that Buddha Nature is ours. It doesn't come from somewhere else." Practicing all the paramitas will encourage us to poke around deep within ourselves until we find that spark. No matter how difficult our personal life may be, no matter how dark the world may seem, if we put forth the effort, if we have the tenacity and courage to just keep sifting the ashes, we will find that glowing ember of hope.

6

Meditating

DHYANA PARAMITA

Drop all relationships, set aside all activities.
Do not think about what is good or evil, and do
not try to judge right from wrong. Do not try
to control perceptions or conscious awareness,
nor attempt to figure out your feelings, ideas, or
viewpoint. Let go of the idea of trying to become
a Buddha as well.

—Dogen Zenji, *Fukanzazengi*

UP TO this point, our discussion of the paramitas has been
centered on how we engage in action with the world in which
we live. With the Paramita of Meditating, we turn toward silent
stillness in the presence of whatever conditions are arising.
My teacher, Joko Beck, often told her students that one of the
reasons we should meditate at least 30 minutes a day is so that
we're awake to what we're doing for the other 23.5 hours of
the day. The world continues unfolding in its perfect array of
joy, sadness, happiness, despair, anxiety, love, hate, death, and
birth. Everything imaginable and unimaginable, everything
seen and unseen—all of it arising and falling away as everything interplays with everything else. And it's just the way it is.
But of course, from our ordinary perspective, the world seems
to revolve around ourselves, our own personal experience of

what's happening, and so it seems of utmost importance that we compare and contrast, pick and choose, accept or reject, cling tightly or push away. It's not obvious or easy to rest in the fundamental rightness and wholeness of each moment, nor can this understanding be reached with our intellect alone. It must be experienced in the silent stillness of mind and body.

The fifth paramita, Meditating, invites us to train in the skill of saying yes to each moment. Even though there are many methods of meditation, such as those intended to relieve stress, cultivate certain mind states, or benefit health, meditation from the perspective of Zen teaching is not a fix or a palliative for difficult states. It places no conditions on anything and rejects nothing, including wanting to reject. It engages us in the act of observing all that rises and falls away in the mind/body. In this way, paradoxically, meditation is hope in action, for we are more often able to engage in whatever conditions we face from the place of clarity that exists beyond the limitation of our self-centered thinking. Zen meditation, or *zazen*, grounds us in stillness and open awareness of the present moment, and it is from this mind that we can meet the world and take wise action. What a different world it would be if just 50 percent of the human population were to pause for five minutes a day to follow their breath in and out, opening to the present moment around them.

What Zen Meditation Is and Isn't

At the door to our Zen center we have a sign that says: "Enter here." On the one hand, the sign simply indicates which door to enter through to get inside our center. However, I like to think of the sign as an invitation to enter into something more—to enter into the fullness of life itself. What I've come to understand, after many years of teaching, is that people enter our doors for all types of reasons. Some are simply seeking a way to feel less stress, perhaps to get some relief from anxiety, depression, or insomnia. Some are coping with serious or chronic illness or loss, while others are struggling through difficult relationships. For some, their curiosity has been piqued by something they read or saw online. Some want to use meditation to reach an altered state of consciousness. And some seekers simply have a nagging sense that something is missing in their life, and so they're on a search. Indeed, meditation techniques can help reduce stress, lower blood pressure, and so forth, and for this reason they are taught in many settings outside of Buddhist practice. But it's important to keep in mind that learning meditation techniques is not the same as engaging in a Zen practice that includes but is not limited to meditation.

It matters not what brings us to the door of entry. What does matter is what happens after we arrive. There aren't any wrong reasons to begin a meditation practice. For some, their early reasons for beginning may blossom into a full immersion into the life of practice; for others, interest may wane until they cease meditating completely. Nevertheless, nothing we do is ever lost, and even just ten minutes of meditating will affect our lives in some way.

Being Just This Moment

> Caught in a self-centered dream, only suffering.
> Holding to self-centered thoughts, exactly the
> dream.

Each moment, life as it is, the only teacher.
Being just this moment, compassion's way.

We often recite the above verse at our Zen center at the end
of our meditation periods. The line "Being just this moment,
compassion's way" is one that is particularly relevant to our
understanding of the Paramita of Meditating and the birth
of hope in each moment. Sometimes meditation in popular
forms is described as "being *in* the moment." However, from
the point of view being discussed here, this phrasing can be
misleading. There is a big difference between being *in* the moment and being *this* moment. Who is it that would be *in* this
moment?

"Just this moment" is simply the perfection of our life no
matter what is arising in a given moment. This is the perfection experienced through zazen. Recently, someone not familiar with meditation asked me what we do when we sit down to
do zazen. I answered: "Just that. We sit down and see what's
up. That's the first thing. No agenda." He quickly responded,
"Oh, I get it. You just let it rip!" Yes, in a way, that's what we
do, but we let it rip in still presence. In the moment, we are
born over and over.

Recently, I was coming out of the supermarket, and as I
turned to place the grocery cart in its bin, I accidently bumped
into a young woman. I turned and apologized, saying, "I'm
sorry. Excuse me." Without skipping a beat, she responded,
saying, "Thank you for this moment to stop!" As our meditation deepens, and the ramblings of self-centered thinking
simmer down, we may experience the moments of our daily
lives—emptying the trash, washing a dish—as the fullness of
what we are. We are nothing more, nothing less, than "this

moment." And within this understanding, we know the hope and power of each and every moment as our life.

Getting Started by Stopping

Learning how to just stop and sit in stillness for five minutes is an extraordinary thing to do for many people. I remember the first time I meditated. I had read a short pamphlet that gave brief instructions for the beginner. The direction was simply to find a quiet place, sit on a chair or on the floor facing the wall, and follow the breath in and out for five minutes. I took my place on the floor cushion, and in just about one minute, I was moved to tears. It hit me like a bolt: I really didn't have to do anything but be there. Just show up. That's all that was being required of me. I was given permission to just be—to just show up, look at the wall, and count my breath. Nothing to prepare in advance, no special state of mind or body I needed to be in. Only the willingness to be there. This type of permission is one we rarely give ourselves, and when I experienced it, it was extraordinary. A voice deep within said, "Ah, yes." But very quickly, of course, it turned into thinking and evaluating my experience. This is what we do. But knowing it's what we do, or doing it without awareness, marks the difference between freedom and imprisonment. So the very first thing we have to learn—and continue learning our whole lives—is simply to just stop in order to meet, with no agenda, whatever is arising in any moment. In time, it becomes a way of life.

Yet even after we've gotten familiar with the feeling of "just stop," the mind will continue to produce thoughts—maybe about whatever we have been doing, about our practice, or about the random topics of mind wandering. But even this kind of thinking can be enfolded into the moment by simply accepting that the mind wants to go off and do all this thinking. It's not that it's wrong or bad. It's simply doing what it is designed to do—think. Just like the birds want to sing and the dog wants to bark. It's okay. This is not to say, however, that we let the mind just spin off. Rather, when we notice that's what's happening, we gently turn our attention toward whatever is arising in that moment, like taking the hand of a small child to guide her in another direction. Over the years, I've grown to appreciate this taking pause and turning attention toward whatever is arising in a given moment. Meditation is not about *getting* somewhere but about *being* where we are— greeting ourselves arriving at our own door. What we most likely will first notice is the busyness of our mind/body. In some moments, it's a very active thinking mind. For others, it may be a squirmy body or emotional energy. What reveals itself when we just stop to greet ourselves is different for all of us each and every time we meditate. What is most important and valuable is not what our experience happens to be, however, but that we turn to meet it.

Zen Meditation: Zazen

Depending on the style and school of meditation, there are various skillful means to help us settle in, strengthen concentration, and deepen meditation. What follows is a general overview of Zen meditation, or zazen, with some limited commentary. Even within the Zen tradition, meditation instructions can vary quite a bit. Zazen meditation usually begins with instructions for following the breath, often with breath counting, as a means to help center and focus the mind/body. Body awareness and sensory input awareness may also be included. It's important to note that even though these types of instruction are given to beginners, in Zen practice, one never graduates beyond their usefulness. We engage in them our whole life.

Many teachers, including myself, are developing more eclectic approaches to meditation instruction by drawing on the rich teachings across the Buddhist traditions. Although one might say there is a risk of "watering down" some of these teachings, I believe that, with care, our access to different styles of meditation can greatly enrich our Western Buddhist meditation tradition. Nevertheless, it's still important for the serious student to seek out a teacher for guidance. Learning from someone with more experience can be critical in differentiating a helpful eclecticism from simply indulging our preferences—the exact opposite of the Zen path. Over time, as we become more skilled, we know what works best for our unique mind/body at a given time.

Posture of Body and Mind

Beginner instruction for Zen meditation usually begins with posture. Most contemporary Zen centers no longer require students to sit in a full lotus position, and it's not uncommon for people to sit in chairs. After many years sitting on the cushion, my aging body sometimes requires a chair. For others, sometimes the body even requires lying down on the floor. What's most important is not the position of our body but the stillness and intimacy of mind and body within that position. Therefore, it's important to begin with a clear understanding of the relationship between posture of the body and posture of the mind. Within the mind/body dynamic, these two postures are intimately related.

Find a quiet place and a comfortable position in a chair or on a cushion. If certain physical conditions prohibit either of these positions, you can lie down or stand up. Keep the eyes open and resting downward at a 45-degree angle. Bring attention to the place where your body touches whatever you're sitting, lying, or standing on and bring to mind the intention to let the body release into the support of the chair, cushion, or floor. Take a few deep breaths and as you exhale think, "let" or "release" into gravity. Shift slowly, moving from the waist in smaller and smaller circles until you begin to sense your center of gravity. Don't worry what it looks like. Focus on what it feels like. Everyone's body is different, and everyone's center of gravity is different. This may take a while to feel, but over time, you'll know when you're letting gravity do its job. Since most of our waking hours are spent in defiance of gravity—standing, walking, or sitting without awareness—when you come into a relaxed alignment with gravity, it'll feel quite light, supported, and effortless.

Our body embodies awareness, and awareness embodies the body. We may think that the purpose of focusing on the correct body posture is so that we can then focus the mind on meditation. However, the mind/body dynamic is much subtler. It allows not even a hair's breadth between the two. Even the slightest unconscious shift of a muscle will change the mind's perception. Even the slightest shift in the mind's focus will cause the body to move with it. It's so subtle that, as we go about our usual daily activities, we don't tend to notice these reciprocal effects. But as we sit in silent stillness, we can begin to notice some of these subtle shifts and holdings, and once those shifts rise into awareness, we can gently release into letting go. The "letting go" I speak of is not, however, permission to scratch an itch or try to shift our bodies for greater comfort but rather a stepping back as we release our holding into simply observing what is present without trying to change or fix it. This, of course, is easier said than done. Anyone who meditates with regularity will have experienced moments in which everything inside screams, "Do something, move, fix it, change it!" But when we can open and allow and release those thoughts, we will have moments when we feel totally balanced, like rocks balanced atop one another—steady without tension, easy without slack. Over time, as we practice bringing awareness toward what we are doing and relinquishing our control, we find a very deep awareness that's always there in the background. To practice the Paramita of Meditating is to invite that awareness to come forward more and more.

The Breath

The first thing we do when we are born is take in a breath. The last thing we do when we die is let go of the breath. Breathing is one of the most fundamental activities we engage in. It supports us in a way nothing and no one else can, and when we observe it, it can calm us and help us see where we are at this moment. The average person breathes 16 breaths per minute while awake and about 6 to 8 while sleeping. That is, on average, 160 breaths per hour or over 23,000 in a 24-hour period. Under stress, the number of breaths can jump to 100 per minute, and it can go as low 4 or 5 per minute in deep meditation. For the purposes of developing our meditation practice, the breath can be very useful. We can think of it as telling our mind, "Okay. You want to put your attention somewhere, so put it here on the breath."

PRACTICE

As you are sitting still, bring your attention to the breath coming in and out. Breathe naturally. You will find that thoughts, feelings, and/or sensations arise. When they do, just note them and bring your attention back to the breath. You can also count the breaths, as described earlier in this chapter. Each time we bring the attention back to breathing, even if we do it a thousand times within a few minutes, our ability to be present deepens, and our resistance to just sitting in the present moment lessens.

Now, starting at the top of your head, slowly wind down your body from head to big toe, bringing awareness to places where you find some holding. It might be helpful to think of the lighthouse beam shining down from the top of your head and spiraling down to your feet, lighting up your awareness.

Just by taking the bodily position and bringing attention to your breathing as described above, the mind will have begun to settle down. But in all likelihood, you'll also begin to notice more subtle thinking, or simply that your mind is very busy. Or you may notice various sensations in the body. This is normal and is going on all the time anyway. The only difference is that right now, you're aware of it.

Often these thoughts or other sensations will send a message to the body to move. It is said that, when the mind moves, the body follows. If you're having a thought such as, "This is boring," you'll likely find that your body is already looking for something to do. It may shift position or begin to fidget. Try to notice when this happens. The point, remember, is to simply take note, observe, and allow. Do not try to maintain some ideal position. Being awake to *how* you are holding your body is much more important than *making* your body stay straight. It takes time for the body to learn to rest in stillness. Busy lives have a way of turning into busy minds and bodies. It takes a while after we exit the freeway for the car to let go of its momentum.

Sometimes this exercise is used as a relaxation technique. However, here we are using it not primarily as a way to relax tensions in the body but rather as way to bring attention to the places we hold in the body and in doing so, sharpen the blade of awareness. When we engage our mind in this way, quite often holdings will relax. If so, that's quite okay. If not, that's also okay. Other times, people will become aware of emotional holdings within the bodily tension. This is a natural occurrence as awareness strengthens.

Noting Thoughts and Emotions

Over time, the longer we practice meditation, the more we realize the ongoing functioning of the mind is to *think*. Thinking is not our problem; our relationship to thinking is. As the ability to settle a bit develops, then techniques to begin labeling thoughts as they rise and fall away and to note body sensations and accompanying emotions may also be included in silent stillness. Koans, the paradoxical phrases or anecdotes commonly drawn from old Chinese or Japanese collections, might be given by the teacher to students as riddles or puzzles intended to help them deepen the capacity to simply be in the complete presence of each moment. But there will always be times when we return again to basic breath counting: one . . . two . . . three. . . .

Usually our thoughts spin like a self-looping tape. Thinking is not bad or even undesirable. What's important is not how many or what type of thoughts we have, but what we do with them. At whatever point in your sitting you notice a thought, take note of its content. It doesn't matter whether it seems important or unimportant. Just label it silently. For example, if you have the thought, "This is boring," then say to yourself, "Having a thought that this is boring." When you notice the mind spinning, just label it, "Having a thought the mind is spinning" or just "Spinning." Then return your attention to breathing.

You may begin to notice that some thoughts have more emotional content than others. This activity of the mind is sometimes called "emotion-thought." For example, a thought such as, "He treated me unfairly" may be accompanied by anger or sadness. Sometimes, you may become aware of the emotion immediately and note the thought sentence that accompanies it later. Whether you experience the thought or the emotion first is of little significance; the important point is simply to be aware of whatever is going on—how that emotion-thought expresses itself in the body.

Sensory Awareness

Emotion-thoughts always have an accompanying sensory experience, whether or not we're awake to it. After a while, you will be more alert to the sensory experience accompanying these emotion-thoughts. For example, if you have a thought like the example above—"He treated me unfairly"—you can label the thought, "Having a thought he treated me unfairly" and then pause for a moment to just follow your breath in and out, keeping the beam of awareness in the body, and with a soft query ask, "Is there an emotion present?" Sometimes, you may feel nothing, even when your intellect thinks you should be feeling something. Other times, you won't even have to query. In fact, you may notice a strong emotion and not even know the thought behind it. This is often the case with anger. Everyone is different, and all situations and holdings are different.

Just Sitting

Most Zen meditation periods last from twenty to forty-five minutes, so it's good to slowly increase your time. Experiencing the deeper levels of zazen require that you sit for an extended period of time. As the mind and body deepen into stillness, we begin letting whatever arises just arise. We stop fighting ourselves and let the mind and body do what they do. If the mind wants to spin off planning, worrying, daydreaming, or whatever, it's not wrong. It's not bad. It's just the nature of the mind to think, just like it's the nature of birds to sing and dogs to bark. When we become aware of the thinking, we just turn our attention toward counting our breaths, feeling the abdomen expand as we breath in. And as the breath releases in the exhalation, feeling the chest and abdomen contract as we silently say, "one, two, three . . ." It's all very relaxed. We're not trying to get somewhere or do something. We become the breathing as mind and body settle down, becoming quieter. Then, perhaps there is a sound in the distance and immediately the attention turns to identify it—a car, a plane, a dog barking. Then we can turn our attention to the sound itself letting it enter our ears, and we hear without listening. And again, in a flash, we're off thinking, planning, judging, and so forth. So we turn to the moment again, rising breath, exhaling, counting . . . Within a five-minute period, our mind can recycle over and over and over. One minute there is nothing but the present moment, and the next, we're remembering something irritating someone said to us an hour ago. Who's keeping track? In time, we come to know meditation is what it is and does what it does, not what we want it to be or what we want it to do. The experienced meditator just notes the thought and perhaps notes if there's an emotive tone to that thought, invites awareness of any body sensations, and turns to the breath. Nothing lost; nothing gained. Just this. Nothing left out.

The point is, meditation is not finding our way into a state of blissful not thinking. It is being totally present to what is arising. We have a choice every time we realize we've wandered off. We can close ourselves up, or we can remember the Paramita of Practicing Patience (presence in what is arising), the Paramita of Engaging Effort (turning energy toward starting again) and the Paramita of Giving and Receiving (giving over and receiving what comes forth). In a split second, the paramitas rise supporting us. We cultivate each of them individually so that in a moment they're there.

Over time, we begin to have moments when thoughts are nothing more than bubbles arising and passing through. Sensations arise in the body. The organs of the eyes, ears, nose, and skin pick up certain data coming through—sound vibrations, scents, prickles of cold air across the face—and awareness just follows as they momentarily pass through. There is just awareness without thinking, without doing anything—"Being just this moment." *We* aren't doing anything. This open awareness is often referred to as *shikantaza*. It's important to understand that it is not a destination in our meditation that we can work toward. In fact, what is most profound is that, while we sense it to be very fundamental and at the core of being, any sense of self has dropped away. People often report an afterthought arising like, "How could I have forgotten this most fundamental perfection?" We haven't gotten anywhere except where we already are but forgot.

Walking Meditation

Even though meditation is most often considered from the point of view of sitting still, the mind of stillness, awareness, and presence can also be experienced while slowly walking. In most Zen centers, periods of sitting meditation are alternated with *kinhin*, walking meditation. As with sitting meditation, the instructions vary depending on the school. However, the primary intention is to experience meditation in motion. During kinhin, we bring awareness to the body as it moves in a slow walk through space.

PRACTICE

Standing with both feet together, without moving forward, begin by slightly moving the weight of the body from one foot to the other. Bring your attention to the feel of the body as it shifts the weight. Notice what various parts of the body do as they respond to your thoughts (whether intentional or unintentional). Now, bring up the intention to move forward—not to walk, but simply to *let* the body move forward. *Let* the foot that is not holding the weight of the body simply lift off the ground. *Letting* rather than *doing* is a very important point, for we are not directing our body to walk, we are simply letting it do what it does naturally when we bring up the intention. As the leg and foot lift and move forward, notice what happens naturally to the other leg when the weight of the body begins to shift. As the moving foot receives the weight, then let the other leg and foot lift and move forward. The movement is slow and continuous. Our hands are either at our sides (if walking on uneven ground) or held loosely at our diaphragm. Our eyes rest gently on the floor or ground in front of us. At first, we will find that our intention wanders, and when that happens, we may find we've begun *directing* ourselves to walk. When you notice this, just bring up the *intention* rather than the *direction* to move forward. Just *let* the body do what it knows how to do. Who is walking?

Commitment and Habit

When we begin doing meditation, we may be enthusiastic and motivated to do it every day. But over time, the newness wears off. This is natural, and though it may seem disappointing, when the "specialness" of meditating has worn away, it is a signal that the deeper work can begin. This juncture is actually a sign that our practice is beginning to deepen and take root. It's a good time to begin personal contact with a teacher and participate in a community of practitioners—a Sangha. But even for people who do find a community of fellow meditators, the choice to meditate every day, even when we don't feel like it—too tired, too busy, too whatever—will be up to us alone. One of the most frequent behaviors when we don't feel motivated or think we're too busy to do our meditation is to put it off. Sometimes, of course, that makes sense, but the most skillful way to deal with procrastination is to just do the meditation and do it *now*, even if it's just for three minutes. The fact is that we always can find time to meditate. It not a question of busyness but rather of intention. Do it for one minute, but do it.

As I noted in the previous chapter, there is a very simple practice I recommend for students who are experiencing reluctance to meditate. Every day, before you begin your routine—before you check email or Facebook, before you get mentally involved with your work or other activities for the day—go to your spot for meditating and stand in front of that spot for a minimum of ten full breaths. You can then go on with other activities or sit down and meditate longer. In time, the mind/body gets used to this activity and will begin to expect it, missing it when you don't do it.

Although it's recommended to have a quiet, private spot in your house where you always do your meditation, it's also important to remember that it can be done in any place. You can do it riding the bus to work. Not being in a special place set aside for meditation is no reason not to take a few moments to stop and tune in to the present moment wherever and however you are. I once had a student who meditated in the bathtub every morning. That's how he started his meditation practice, in his hot bath. And then slowly he moved out of the bathtub onto a cushion. But it was the only place in his tiny house where he could find a place where people wouldn't disturb him. These days, there are many Dharma talks and guided meditations available online, and these can be used as a stimulus to your practice. However, joining a local Zen center and practicing with others is invaluable. In Buddhist teaching, the community of practitioners, the Sangha, is considered one of the Three Jewels along with Buddha and Dharma. Make a commitment to yourself to attend regularly. Tell the people there to expect you. Ask if you can have an obligation like unlocking the door or arranging cushions and chairs, so that the commitment will support you. By giving your time and effort, you will receive the gift of the Sangha. Each of us must make the choice of how we want to live. If we choose not to meditate, that's our choice. It's not about being right or wrong, good or bad. It's simply being open and honest about how we want to engage in this life—that's all.

STUDENT SHARING

Student: Could you speak more about the difference or transition from breath counting to what you call "just sitting" or "just being?"

Diane: Every meditation period is different, but we will experience times when the mind settles down, and there's no need to count. Rather than us doing something, a sense of an observer arises in silent stillness. Thoughts may arise, bubbling through, and then just disappear without turning into internal narrative. Sounds enter through the ears, and other sensations float through. Perhaps there is some physical or emotional energy that arises. There's simply observing, watching whatever rises and falls away. My teacher, Joko, once described this aspect of meditation like sitting on the edge of a pin. Not to be confused with an altered state of bliss or leaving the body, but simply complete awareness within the stillness.

Student: So would you typically start out with the counting and then just see where it goes? Or does it really just depend on the day?

Diane: It depends on the day and the many conditions known and unknown that are cocreating our experience. Our intention is to just show up.

Student: I have been meditating for a number of years now, and it's only recently that I realized that I very much had it in my mind that a real period of meditation was a minimum of thirty minutes long. So there would be some days when I don't sit because I don't have that much time. I think if I'm really going to do it, it should be forty-five minutes really, but thirty-five is okay . . . And I'll think about, say, how my evening is playing out and what I need to do, and there's not that chunk of time, and so I don't sit. And it's really only recently that I realized that's just a requirement that I legislated for myself. That ten minutes of sitting is ten minutes of sitting. And there could be ten minutes in the morning and ten minutes in the evening, ten minutes here and ten minutes there, fifteen minutes here, but the important thing is that I sit when I can and not feel like I have to have a big chunk of time.

Diane: Your point is important to keep in mind. It's never all or nothing. Also, as I mentioned elsewhere, our formal periods of meditation help us be awake to what's going on when we're not meditating. Mindful awareness can pop in anywhere. It can pop in while you're waiting for a light to turn green. It can pop in while you're waiting for a computer to connect to something. Standing in line at the grocery store. Watching a pot of tea brew. Being caught in traffic while late for an appointment. Instead of growing frustrated and spinning off into various kinds of thinking when the stoplight is too slow, you can take a mini moment to just turn to your breath and meet yourself arriving right there. And in that moment, you are also engaging in the Paramita of Practicing Patience. Whatever your situation, find a way to take "cat sits" throughout the day. Go to the bathroom. Sit in the toilet and do a cat sit. Really. You're in the doctor's office or waiting on the phone to hear test results. Turn that moment into a brief meditation.

Student: I was doing that recently when I was interviewing for a job, and they were sending in three people at a time to interview me. It was a really hot day, and I had a wool suit on.

It was really intense because there was no way to prep for the next interviewer in any way. The worst thing I could do was to start to think about what I was going to say because I didn't even know who was coming through the door and had no idea what they'd ask me. I didn't know the context, so there was no way I could spin anything. So, for the moments in between each interview, I followed my breath. I turned to the sounds in the adjoining office. I let whatever was in the environment enter into my awareness. I felt totally present and realized that's all the prep I needed to then carry on responding to their questions.

Diane: There's really no timetable or progress to speak of in our Zen practice. Don't be surprised if some or all of this doesn't come easily. People have different experiences, not just in beginning meditation practice, but even twenty, thirty, forty, fifty years later. It's always changing, and there's always something new to discover about our self-creating as we sit in the silent stillness of meditation. When we begin to purposely stop and pay attention to our body, our breath, our thoughts, we are becoming more intimate with ourselves. Some may feel calm, centered, relaxed while others may have trouble just sitting still for a couple of minutes. Over time, however, whatever our experience in the beginning, the "specialness" of meditation will wear away, and we will begin to notice more and more subtle aspects of mind and body. This can often be troubling. For example, we may notice that the initial calm and relaxation may turn to agitation. We may notice bodily sensations that we were never aware of before or notice how our minds are continually spinning. These experiences, if not understood as a sign of growing awareness, can be discouraging and cause us to think, "It's not working." This is when working with a teacher is very helpful. Remember, the purpose of meditating every day is not limited to the meditation experience itself but also includes our waking up to what we're doing when we're not meditating. This potential for seeing clearly is, without question, within all of us. So we are not trying to *get* something. Rather we are *cultivating* what is ours simply by recognizing it. This seeing clearly is what we call "wisdom" and is what arises as we practice all the paramitas. In time, you will find, if even for only the briefest of moments, you can be awake and fully present to whatever comes your way.

7

Seeing Clearly

Prajna Paramita

Except for the point, the still point
There would be no dance, and there is only the
dance.
—T. S. Eliot, *Burnt Norton*, "The Still Point"

MANY YEARS ago, I was walking by a river with my teacher, Joko Beck. We crossed a small footbridge, and as we looked down into the whirlpools of water, Joko commented: "How like our life. We whirl around the rocks and debris and mistake the whirlpool we're caught in as all of life. We don't see that we're really the whole of the river." Later, in her book *Nothing Special*, she wrote the following:

> We are rather like whirlpools in the river of life. In flowing forward, a river or stream may hit rocks, branches, or irregularities in the ground causing whirlpools to spring up spontaneously here and there. Water entering one whirlpool quickly passes through and rejoins the river, eventually joining another whirlpool and moving on. Though for short periods it seems to be distinguishable

as a separate event, the water in the whirlpools is just the river itself. The stability of a whirlpool is only temporary. The energy of the river of life forms living things—a human being, a cat or dog, trees and plants—then what held the whirlpool in place is itself altered, and the whirlpool is swept away, reentering the larger flow. The energy that was a particular whirlpool fades out and the water passes on, perhaps to be caught again and turned for a moment into another whirlpool.[1]

What strikes me most about the words above is that not once is the word "wisdom" used. Rather, what is described is an ongoing, moving life force that runs through and transforms everything from humans to dogs, trees, and plants. In the Zen tradition, we call it *prajna*, wisdom. We might refer to it as "deeper intelligence," "creative force," or numerous other names, but its true reality is beyond names and is simply manifested in its expression in the world. Whatever it is called, it is all that forms the whirlpool as well as the river itself. It is all that creates the flies and fish, as well as our fishy, buzzing human lives. It is vast, open, inexplicable nothingness that flows through and with all existence, appearing spontaneously and offering no hint about where to find it or exactly what it is. If we search for it or try to define it, it eludes us, and yet it is revealed in and through all things. The Paramita of Seeing Clearly is the raft, the shore, and the oceanic depths on which we float and paddle. This last paramita teaches that there is no permanent entity we can call me, you, it, or them. There is only arising and falling away in each and every moment.

If this vast, ungraspable, and ineffable open awareness is the fundamental nature of reality, how can we engage in the practice of the Paramita of Seeing Clearly? If there is nothing to attain, how can we even seek? Zen teachers throughout the ages have reminded us that although what we speak of here is fundamentally present within us all, it only manifests through living our everyday lives. Seeing clearly with the eye of prajna wisdom is not a concept or something we can grasp through our minds. It may be realized in moments of meditation, but it is only manifested in our actions in the world. So, even though practicing the paramitas won't lead us to the final destination—the realization of wisdom—they can serve as the vessel to bring it forth into the world.

Creation of Our World

As our meditation deepens, and the ramblings of self-centered thinking simmer down and disappear, we may begin to have glimpses of this ever-so-subtle mystery beyond our unique ways of perceiving anything. Whether a glass of water, the sound of a bird, a screeching tire, the smell of smoke, sharp words from a loved one, the most recent violence reported on the news, things we did or did not do in the past or that we might or might not do in the future—we may begin to glimpse that each and all of these are based on an inconceivable confluence of known and unknown factors.

Imagine you are walking down a country road at night. You look down at the ground and suddenly see a snake and become frightened. Then you turn on your flashlight and shine it on the ground. You look again and see that there is only a rope, no snake. The rope was there all along—it was never a snake—but the rope appeared to be a snake because your sight was obscured by the darkness, because you did not focus your light on it. When you thought you were seeing a snake, you became filled with fear and worry, but when you found that it was only a rope, the appearance of the snake dissolved. In the traditional telling of this story as a Dharma teaching, the snake is a metaphor for the self or ego, the flashlight stands for wisdom, or Seeing Clearly, and the rope is the process, including our senses and perceptions, that creates what we believe to be reality. These senses and perceptions are often referred to as the "five *skandhas*" or aggregates. The five skandhas are a way of looking at what constitutes our experience of each moment. I like to express them as follows:

1. *Form/physicality/matter.* This is the material form of an experience that comes in through our eyes seeing, ears hearing, nose smelling, tongue tasting, skin touching, and mind thinking. In the darkness, we see a snake, our feet touch something, or perhaps we smell or hear something.

2. *Sensations.* This is sometimes described as the flavor that accompanies the physical/material form. The flavor arises before thought and is generally categorized as pleasant, neutral, or unpleasant. Before any thoughts or narratives have even formed, we already feel attraction to a pleasant sensation or aversion to an unpleasant sensation or association with the information received from the senses.

3. *Perceptions.* This is the experience of our knowing we are having an experience. There's a cognition that takes place. *I* am experiencing this pleasant, unpleasant, or neutral feeling, *and* I believe it's true because *I* am experiencing it. Although it may not be true, the sensations received are making me feel

pleasant, neutral, or uncomfortable, and I attach to my interpretation of those feelings. This is sort of a knee-jerk reaction to what the eyes, ears, and so forth come in contact with.

4. *Mental formations (sometimes referred to as "volition").* This is our reaction to the experience. What is my reaction to what I see on the ground? Do I cry out? Jump back?

5. *Consciousness.* This skandha takes the previous four and combines them into a recursive whole: "I am a self having this experience, and because I am having this experience, I am a self." Consciousness includes every-thing from the most fundamental input we have from our senses to the feelings and thoughts we have about those perceptions, including distant past memories and associations.

It's important to keep in mind that although these skandhas are listed in a serial order, they really arise in nanoseconds and are constantly interweaving with each other. The other impor-tant point to keep in mind is the words of the *Heart Sutra* reminding us that all the skandhas are *empty*—meaning they have no enduring life but rise in a moment and then fall away.

The skandhas coalesce in a moment and create our perceptions and view of our life. As they whirlpool together, they govern how we live our life and how we engage in the world. There is an opportunity to relieve suffering through understanding how this works for each of us and also how it functions for groups and even whole nations. All human experience, all of our individual and collective whirlpools, are formed from these components.

Not only are our perceptions colored by what is happening in this present moment—such as the words written on this page entering through the sense organ of your eyes, and your mental processing gears going into motion—but also, as part of that mechanism, there's whatever feelings arise as a result of those words. So our perceptions, how we create reality and try to make sense of the world, are colored also by our mental formations. It's like putting water into a square jar. Under certain conditions, the water may freeze into a square and won't become liquid until the condition of the freezing temperature is changed. But if you've never experienced water that's not frozen, you may think that the nature of water is that it's always frozen. This conditioned thinking determines how we perceive other people, things, and events—it's a fundamental step in our creation of "self." Please note that I'm not only referring here to personal psychological history, our upbringing and individual experiences, but of history that goes back millions of years and is, in a sense, beginningless.

Carlo Rovelli, a quantum physicist, describes the human self as "a huge wave of happenings. . . . Our senses convey a picture of reality that narrow our understanding of its fullness."[2] Feeling the weight and density of this book and seeing the shape of it in your hands filters through perceptions and past associations that lead you to the conclusion that this is, indeed, a book and that it exists separately from you. But suppose our normal life span wasn't ninety or so years, but rather more like a billion years? This book, then, would be just a moment in which some molecules come together and then disintegrate. What we call a book is really just a momentary getting together of certain kinds of particles and fibers.

Buddhist teacher Stephen Batchelor, in describing how we come to identify ourselves (and others), writes:

We too are impressions left by something that used to be here. We have been created, molded, formed by a bewildering matrix of contingencies that have preceded us. From the patterning of the DNA derived from our parents to the firing of the hundred billion neurons in our brains to the cultural and historical conditioning of the twentieth century to the education and upbringing given us to all the experiences we have ever had and choices we have ever made: these have conspired to configure the unique trajectory that culminates in this present moment. What is here now is the unrepeatable impression left by all of this, which we call "me." Yet so vivid and startling is this image that we confuse what is a mere impression for something that exists independently of what formed it. . . .

As we become aware of all this, we can begin to assume greater responsibility for the course of our lives. Instead of clinging to habitual behavior and routines as a means to secure this sense of self, we realize the freedom to create who we are. Instead of being bewitched by impressions, we start to create them. Instead of taking ourselves so seriously, we discover the playful irony of a story that has never been told in quite this way before.[3]

Moments of Insight

The most common descriptions in Zen literature of moments of seeing clearly are short stories or examples of meditators who, in the process of doing meditation for a long period of time, experience a moment when the whirlpool releases, the self-identity drops away, and there is just open awareness beyond the mind, which separates and categorizes. This experience is often described as "emptiness." But it's important to remember that this is not what we may think of as an empty void. This falling away of "self" holds all of life itself, including our life within the world with all our happiness, laughter, tears, and sadness. Our practice is to experience all we do as human beings but to do so without holding on to anything. This "not holding on" is emptiness.

The power of this emptiness allows us to move from an illusory dream of self to an experience of life that knows no boundary. Common words cannot describe it, so it is often phrased metaphorically ("show me the place of no heat and no cold") or with images ("the bottom fell out of the bucket"). When these experiences occur, the meditator, in that moment, understands beyond an intellectual comprehension of the teachings—beyond whirlpools and rivers, being and nonbeing, yes/no, right/wrong, heat/cold.

Oftentimes, when a person has such a moment, they'll then try to hold on to that insight, tossing yet one more piece of debris into their whirlpool. A wise teacher will see this and offer them the chance to break through.

Take, for example, this Zen koan: A student came to the teacher and said, "I'd like to tell you about an experience of seeing clearly that I had yesterday." The teacher pointed to the door and said, "Please go wash out the garbage cans in the yard. I can smell them all the way in here."

For some people, spontaneous moments of insight arise even without any experience of meditation. A friend who had no experience of Zen or meditation once described to me an experience she had when she was in a city subway station waiting for a train on a hot summer day: "It was sweltering hot, and it was the rush-hour commute. People were jammed next to each other, and tempers were beginning to flare. A fight broke out between two young men whose anger was like fire. I placed myself between their two bodies, and as I looked up into the face of the man closest to me, my own face was before me. In that split second, we were not two but one."

These types of spontaneous openings allow us to experience the fullness of life itself, beyond the limits of our personal projections. Usually it lasts for only a short time, but nevertheless some part of us gets a nudge that there's a lot more to all of this than we may think we know. All too often, however, the moment of insight is forgotten, and wisdom as action arising out of seeing clearly is not reflected in our daily living.

Wisdom of Don't Know

A Zen story tells of a young seeker who, after studying the teachings for some time, packs up his books and travels from teacher to teacher to gather more knowledge. When he arrives at one temple, he's invited to have tea with the teacher, which is the custom for visitors. He sits down at the table where two empty cups and a full teapot are laid out. After some initial introductory comments, the student commences a long discourse about his expertise with Zen practice. At that point, the teacher picks up the teapot and fills her own cup with tea and then places the pot on the table without filling the visitor's cup. They sit in silence for a while, and when her cup is empty, she refills her cup and, again, neglects to fill the young man's cup. By this time, the young man is perplexed and says, "I have truly enjoyed sitting here with you, but why have you not poured tea into my empty cup?" The teacher answered, "Your cup is already brimming over. There's no room for anything else." What the teacher in this story is pointing out to the young seeker is that the gateway to seeing clearly is to realize that we really don't know a lot.

Seeing clearly means that we first need to recognize that all that we think we know is but a limited perspective, and that our perspectives are formed by an infinite array of conditions including but not limited to the mechanisms of our own body and mind. We are not and never will be omniscient, although we may conduct our lives as if we are. We've all had those moments when we realize we were off and running with our thoughts and judgments and didn't see something very obvious. This sort of tunnel vision is how the human mechanism of perception functions. We don't necessarily really know what's happening at this moment with our neighbor behind the closed door of their house or with the world leader thousands of miles away. Yet, we certainly act like we know everything! And therein lies the source of our delusions. Not that we can't know it all, but that we *think* we know it all. Thus, we're reminded again of the importance of the teaching, "don't know." A good way to access this perspective is simply to develop the habit of asking yourself, "Is that so?"

Stepping Forth into the World

> When I see I am nothing, that is wisdom. When I see I am everything, that is enlightenment. My life is a movement between the two.
> —Nisargadatta Maharaj, *I Am That*

The Zen literature is abundant with stories of practitioners for whom the "self" has dropped away into open awareness or emptiness. In the words of the *Heart Sutra*, no eyes, ears, nose, tongue, or body remain. In some teachings, this event is considered a milestone in one's practice, for this glimpse of nothingness brings to light the realization that all we assume to be the totality of living is naught but a fragment of a greater whole. But wisdom, or Seeing Clearly, has two aspects: seeing clearly into the vast, open expanse of no-self *and* manifesting this insight as action in the world. No matter what experiences we have through our practice, we must reenter the world to benefit others as well as ourselves. We must release our grip on any experience of "attainment" and step back into the fray of the world to take action informed by an understanding that is both beyond and including self and other. This will be different for each of us, depending on what we can offer in the spirit of giving. It is through the practice of the paramitas that we will find our own way.

Simply put, on the one hand, we are inescapably interconnected in the vast, open river (even though we may not realize it) and, on the other hand, we are temporary constructs of a mind and body that we call "self." We are the whirlpool and we are the river. In Zen terms, we are form and vast emptiness; self and no-self.

When the boundary of self drops away, the perfection of everything and the reality of interconnectedness is clearly seen. What all Zen practice helps us understand is that the fundamental connection of everything is what underlies all our experience—me and you, this or that. Far beyond the philosophical implications, I think a serious look at how our perceptions work is of extreme importance in today's world. The problems we face as a planet—environmentally, politically, socially, and economically—call for us to address our interdependence on all levels. We may think, "What can I, as one person, do in the face of the powers that be?" But when you think on it, interconnectedness means that even my smallest actions affect the world. So, to understand first that our view of reality is governed by a complex matrix of perceptions is essential. We can and should take action, but we must also tend to our personal, unique way of coming to what we believe is true. In this way, don't-know mind is, in and of itself, a political stance. It requires an open inquiry in which we let go of certainty, understanding what is true not from our limited perceptions but from seeing things as they are. When I think I "know," and the person holding a different view doesn't "know," then our interaction can only be confrontational. However, when we bear witness, listening with an open heart and open mind, then whatever action we take will be transformative. This takes great courage and great fortitude, for it's much easier to stand firm in our personal views of things than to truly be open to transformation by standing firm in the power of what best serves life. The former is standing within the boundaries of our own (and perhaps our group's) view of "truth." The latter includes our view but is not limited to it; it calls for us to stand in the middle of a greater circle of beings and groups, even those who are unknown to us.

STUDENT SHARING

Student: My question about don't-know mind relates to how we can take action in the world such as "political action" without a sense of "knowing" that something should be different. I "know" for sure that bombing civilians is wrong, as is mistreatment of people of different ethnicities, racial backgrounds, religions, and genders, as well as all the numerous other ways we separate *us* from *them*. I know that sometimes we need to say "NO! This is wrong!"—whether it's to our partner, our kids, our coworkers, or to society as a whole. How can I do this without "knowing"?

Diane: History has born witness to people who have stepped forward with strong voices arising out of this don't-know mind. This taking action beyond self-centeredness stems from a true understanding of the fundamental goodness of everyone. However, as I say, this is not simple or easy. It requires deep commitment and especially the practice of all the paramitas, which help keep us afloat and clear in the troubled waters of our life. The paramitas bring us to the awareness that our sense of what's true has come through a matrix of interweaving conditions. Through the Paramita of Meditating, and in the spirit of the open inquiry of don't-know mind, we can just observe that "felt sense" inviting clear seeing, or wisdom, to arise. We're aware that the felt sense that's coming through the hearing of the ears, the seeing of the eyes, the words of that person speaking, may or may not be right or true. How we react to the way that person is speaking may or may not be right. It may be our perception, but it may not be accurate. Over time, we can see our personal experience in a less personal way. This is sometimes referred to as nonattachment and leads us into wise action.

CONCLUSION:
BEYOND THE WHIRLPOOL

GIVEN ALL that we face in our personal lives as well as this world of the twenty-first century, we can either fall into a spiral of hopeless despair, or we can turn toward cultivating a way of seeing clearly. All that we think we are, all that we think makes this world, is but a little momentary whirlpool that comes together and falls apart. The important role of the paramitas is that they remind us that how we live our life and how we engage in the world is integral to the shape and form of each of our whirlpools. We and all that we love and hate, fear and welcome are interconnected oneness. And the *seeing* is revealed spontaneously within our actions, before even a *thought* of wisdom arises—like the flow of the river, the gathering of moss and stones into an eddy, the cry of a newborn, the scream of a dying soldier, the tears of joy, and the spontaneity of laughter.

Net of Indra

An ancient Buddhist text, the *Avatamsaka Sutra*, conceives the universe as an enormous net—Indra's net—that extends infinitely in all directions, protecting and nurturing all of life and excluding nothing. Each juncture in the net is home to a shiny, multifaceted, reflective jewel. Because of its many sides, each jewel reflects every other jewel in an infinite network of mutual support of each other's existence. It's difficult to imagine the countless number of jewels in a net this size, let alone the endless number of reflections on each jewel. No jewel exists without the other jewels. No jewel stands alone. All are dependent on the presence of others. If one appears, all appear; if one does not appear, none appear. If you were to place one black dot on any one of the jewels, it would appear in all the jewels.

Indra's net is a compelling image illustrating unceasing, unobstructed interpenetration and mutual interdependence of all existence. Every action, every word, every thought—our memories, desires, fears, urges, frustrations, happiness, peace, and well-being—ripples its effect into the universe. No one and nothing is excluded in this mutual resonance and all-inclusive relationship. As Vietnamese Zen master Thich Nhat Hanh reminds us, we carry in our heart not only our personal joys and sorrows, but also the joys and sorrows that are society itself. When you take action that brings about well-being for yourself, you bring about well-being for the world. When you take action that is harmful to yourself, you bring harm into the world. All of life is one, and all things and events are part of this invisible wholeness. Receiving and giving to ourselves with open hands and heart, connecting by practicing patience in our experience of the moment, taking skillful action based on our inherent vow to recognize all of life, grounding ourselves in strength and fortitude, pausing in stillness to allow a deeper intelligence to inform our steps—the practice of the paramitas affects the world in ways we cannot measure or perhaps even see. Yet, it is true. To follow the teaching of the paramitas is taking harmonious action with the interrelatedness of all things. It is a way of living and practicing in accord with the view that every action has an effect and every effect leads to a cause in an infinite web of life.

Meeting "me as everything" isn't what comes naturally to most of the world. For most of us, our view of life is fairly narrow and confined within the boundaries of what serves our self-identity—the dream that life centers on me. This is why we need our practice. In fact, the longer we practice, the more we begin to see the ever-so-subtle ways in which the construction of self narrows our view of others. If we sincerely want to touch a deeper truth about who we are and how we are all interconnected into something greater, into life itself, then we'll need to bring to light the ways in which we can quite innocently and subtly become entrapped in perceptions of separation.

How subtly and quickly the sense of "I and other" rises up. It's hard even to note what happens first—what we take in physically through our senses, the perceptions that arise, the predispositions that occur before thinking, and finally the thoughts. These all occur sort of together, like a big bang. And this all happens at the level of preconception, you might say the subconscious level, before we have formed belief systems and so forth—before we even identify ourselves with a particular group—race, ethnicity, gender, and so forth. As we've discussed in previous chapters, it's an essential part of our practice to cultivate a crystal-clear awareness of this microscopic construction of self, and it's also very useful and important to approach this self-making from the macroscopic view of how we build and maintain this identity in relation to others.

If I have a certain color skin, certain type of eye shape,

belong to a particular cultural or ethnic group, speak a certain language, or express my connection with gender in a certain way, then commonly I will also identify myself as *inside* that group, and those who don't share any of these things are *outside* my identity group. It's not a question of liking or disliking but of separation itself—me and you or us and them. As Mother Teresa reminded us, we have drawn our circle too small. We all have stories about our experiences in any of these groups. And hearing others' stories is important, keeping in mind that each group will experience its own expressions of inclusion and exclusion. Viewed from the perspective of self and other, uncovering our own stories and encouraging others to do the same can be enormously helpful in widening our circle.

PRACTICE

Zen practitioners, who are steeped in the teaching of inclusiveness in the great, vast river of oneness, may fool themselves into thinking they've already accepted difference in others. But the voice of vast inclusiveness also speaks to the everyday whirlpools of us and them. This is where the Paramitas of Meditating and Engaging Effort are very important, for this exploration requires cultivating strong effort, a keen awareness of mind/body, and fortitude to face our deepest holdings. This work requires much more than a cursory exploration, for our biases are ever so subtle. Most important is to have the intention to observe closely how you see yourself in relation to others who are "different" from your identity group. Although this first step may seem obvious, it can be very elusive. For example, you may notice a slight physical sensation on seeing the physical presentation of another, as in the first skandha of physical form, which includes anything that the sense organs take in. Or perhaps you first notice a feeling or a thought. It takes but a nanosecond of recognition.

When you recognize something is happening, allow your awareness to rest in observing its unfolding. Here, the Paramita of Practicing Patience arises. Is there a bodily sensation of tightness, openness, cold, heat? Is there an emotion—fear, anger, guilt, or happiness? What about thoughts—are you hearing reruns of old stories, either pleasurable or unpleasurable? It's not important to note which of these things you recognize first. Just let whatever your awareness catches be the portal to further exploration, allowing the experience to be what it is. Just meet it with openness and soft curiosity, not demanding any answers or resolution. This is a lot easier said than done because judging-mind thoughts will quickly want to censor or encourage other experiences, and it takes a great deal of courage to face our experience in this way. Much of our life of Buddhist practice is devoted to the special kind of allowing whereby we cultivate the ability to just be an observer of the present moment in open awareness. If you identify yourself as a member of a group of people who believes they carry no racial, ethnic, or gender bias against any other group, then it may be very hard to pick up on the subtler levels of perception and memory skandhas that reach deep into our psyche, far beyond our present life experience. It may be very difficult to allow the discovery that, like nearly everyone in our culture, you *are* carrying forms of bias or prejudice. This point can't be overstated. It is extremely subtle for those of us in Zen practice. Returning again to the river and the whirlpool can be helpful here. While we can, in our personal and group practices, make every attempt to be all inclusive, there will always be no distinction and no differences, and there will always be distinctions and differences. The paramitas remind us that we are always on the raft, always paddling, always getting caught in the tempests and the doldrums. We need to stay awake! Pay attention! Never assume we've arrived. And when we live our life in this way, we find the shore is always appearing right under our feet.

From inside the experience, label what you are experiencing. Perhaps you notice a slight pulling away, a tinge of extra vigilance. Again

I emphasize, don't push. A label may not appear right away. If that happens, just stay in a place of bearing witness for a few moments. I sometimes suggest a very light whiff of questioning—*What is this?* or *What is this like?* Especially, no demands for answers. This takes a great deal of Practicing Patience. You may notice particular thoughts or sensations (including sensations of energies like sexual energy, anger energy, or warm heart energy), emotions, feeling tones, tensing, or relaxing in areas of the body. Whatever is being experienced, let the awareness become intimate with it, and see if it labels itself. Just breathe and watch as intensity rises and falls away. Notice if there are spaces in between, and if so, allow the awareness to include those spaces and pause there.

Engage the Paramita of Taking Skillful Action, which will emerge out of and through this self-inquiry. Taking action that nurtures inclusion, that drops the barrier of self and other, doesn't always happen quickly. Like everything else, we need to engage the support of all the paramitas. But in time, moments of skillful action will occur from the heart and not just from a proper "stance." You'll know it when it happens, for there will be no question—no confusion about the right words to say or the correct thing to do—all of that is just another form of conditioning.

STUDENT SHARING

Student: How do you face squarely the facts of what's happening in the world we live in today and still have even a smidgeon of optimism, let alone hope that in the end we'll survive it all?

Diane: We can only do what we think supports life and see what happens. We never truly know anything we think we know and to understand this *don't know* is the opening to seeing clearly. Today, the clouds are in the sky, and we see no sun shining through. Yet, we all agree that the sun is behind those clouds and once the clouds separate, it will appear. But do we really know that? Since that question is scary, in our collective mind, we hang on to what our past experience has shown us: clouds disperse and sun appears. Of course, we must live our life on this planet assuming there is a sun behind the clouds, but a Zen master might ask, "Is that so?" All kinds of possibilities reside in "don't know."

Student: Don't know for me is like riding a seesaw, especially in relation to my personal choices of action around climate change. I have chosen to take strong action in my personal life, so I drive a car that burns vegetable oil. I have solar panels to provide all the electricity in my house. I wear a headlight at night instead of turning on lights that would drain the power grid. In fact, I'm a bit nutsy about energy conservation. Then I see people driving SUVs, and once I get over my initial judgment of that person driving such a gas guzzler by engaging in the Paramita of Taking Skillful Action, specifically, letting go of the anger and meeting them on equal ground, sometimes a little voice comes forward and asks, "How do you know what you're doing is really going to be better for the planet?" Now, of course, I know it's good to pay attention to my carbon footprint and do whatever I can in my personal life, but what can I really know when we consider that we ultimately don't know what the future will bring. Sometimes I joke with people that the purpose of humanity is to pull all the fossil fuels out of the ground so that the dinosaurs can have the planet back! Then they can eat all the ferns, carbon, and heat, and we humans will be out of their way! Then I realize, I don't really know if all my energy-saving activities are really supporting life, helping the planet survive. For whose purpose? If I ask a dinosaur, I might get a surprising answer. At the same time, however, it feels right to me, indeed, like wise action, to do what I'm doing, even if I'm just helping humanity to be free of dinosaurs. So my question is, "Can't we get so caught in don't-know mind that we become paralyzed?" If prajna wisdom is to see clearly and then to take action from that, how can we see clearly if we don't know?

Diane: First, it's important to remember that *don't know* doesn't mean don't act. It means to act wisely. To take wise action is to take action that arises out of seeing clearly that there are many conditions present and that we can't possibly know them all. This is vastly different from choosing to live a life of energy conservation from a rigidly unyielding perspective. Can we imagine what a different world this would be if more people released holding on to their individual and group "truths"? The Paramita of Seeing Clearly supports us in this way by first helping us release our self-centered views and then taking action from a larger, open perspective that includes but is not limited to those views.

What I notice quite a bit in my own thinking, when I take the swing into despair and, yes, sometimes name calling, is that my perception has narrowed. My view of the situation or the person I'm judging has become contracted and closed. I have lost intimacy. And to be honest, there's a strange kind of what I call "false strength" or "false control" that accompanies that enclosure. But, of course, the narrowing just draws in tighter and tighter, creating an illusion of control when, in fact, it's the opposite. It's the opposite because I'm leaving out what is seen and unseen. I have lost intimacy. Our perceptions are quite limited and quite automatic. They're all we have, though, to live in this world. Seeing Clearly acknowledges that whatever we are perceiving is not the whole picture and to take the wisest action we can based on the fact that we can never know it all. I think in times like this, especially when we feel little hope, we can all remind ourselves of the practice of "don't know it all; can't know it all; there's more than meets the eye here." But don't know doesn't mean a shrug of the shoulders or resignation. The practice of don't know is the opposite of resignation. First it challenges us to face the limitations of what we "think" we know and that's not so easy. What comes up when we relinquish or even just doubt our certainty? Secondly, when we open the mind to don't know, we are then free to look and see more openly. This can be quite freeing, and we can see things in new and creative ways. Don't know leaves a door of possibility open. We widen our perceptions. We leave a crack for the light to shine in. We allow intimacy.

All of Zen practice invites and encourages us to let go of what we think we know, including who we think we are, and instead open our hearts and minds to what is truly before us— to truly see and hear the person shouting offensive slogans during a political rally before taking action; to look deeply into the person struggling on the streets by truly being there, present without all we *think* we know—our views, our judgments, and so forth. Perhaps we remember the Paramita of Dana, giving freely of all that we can, or Practicing Patience, allowing the events to unfold, or any of the other paramitas. The experience may only last for a moment, but in that moment, the wisdom inherent within all things comes forward. And in the moment, we find ourselves standing on the other shore.

It Ain't Over Till It's Over

In the words of the great American baseball player, Yogi Berra, "It ain't over till it's over." As I enter my seventy-fifth year of life and fourth decade of Zen practice, I think I might finally be getting the message! I'm also reminded of something Zen master Yasutani Roshi said: "It took me twenty years to realize enlightenment, and it will take me the rest of my life to manifest it." I would add "to ripen."

My whole life, I've been a person with lots of energy. Over the past years, however, because of age and conditions known and unknown to me, that energy has diminished. And along with it, that person with a lot of energy, that "can do" identity, has diminished. No longer can I be that person. And not only has that energy diminished, but also I find when I don't pay attention to the here and now—open, listen, receive, take skillful action—the other conditions get triggered. So how do I meet this? One way is to say, "It's over. I just can't do any of this anymore. Game over." But is the game over, or have the rules just changed? And if the rules have changed, how do I learn these new rules so that I can stay awake in the game?

At any age, when the rules of "our" game change, we can come close to just giving up, and how sad is that when all we have to do is wake up to our life, right now? Another way might be to find new strategies to assure energy. This could serve to maintain a lively identity. But this doesn't necessarily work. One day, sleeping, eating, exercising in a certain way I may feel abundant energy; another day, with the same regime, my energy plummets. So what do I have to depend on? Nothing but right here, right now. And what's the best course of action to take given the conditions right here and right now? At our Zen center, we often chant the words: "Just this moment; compassion's way." Just this moment, including perhaps terror, but also potentially liberation. For in truth, "just this moment" is the only moment and being open to it is the only true choice we ever really have. We suffer when we try to get around it.

This is what bringing the paramitas into our life offers us—they keep us on the true course to our inherent capacity to live fully by meeting uncertainty and change with openness and possibility. They offer us a way to respond to life and stay in the game. It ain't over; it's just changing. They encourage us to just show up, opening our hands to receive what is coming forward and letting go of what we cling to—the Paramita of Giving and Receiving. They encourage us to give attention to the actions we take, to consider whether they stem from wisdom and compassion or from self-centered thinking—the Paramita of Taking Skillful Action. They encourage us toward our deepest human capacities, such as the capacity to rest in and observe whatever is arising, allowing it to run its course—the Paramita of Practicing Patience. They encourage us to consider what kind of effort we're making, and how we place our energy in the midst of it all—the Paramita of Engaging Effort. They encourage us to set aside time to meet ourselves in quiet stillness just as we are—the Paramita of Meditating. The paramitas lead us to see things clearly, without the contortions of our self-centered grasping—the Paramita of Seeing Clearly.

Over time, as we ripen, we are more and more able to meet situations that we might have considered a burden as opportunities to engage. The key is that the paramitas are not something *out there*. They are deep within all of us at the core of our being, and they're always there to serve us. Something changes, something is different when we invite them forth. Then we greet life as it knocks on our door; we invite it in and we keep on going—it ain't over. Nothing is ever over; everything just changes. All is changing. It's so simple. We can only ripen into what is now. And therein lies hope.

Notes

Introduction

1. Václav Havel, *Disturbing the Peace* (New York: Vintage Books, 1990), 181–82.

Chapter 1: What Are the Paramitas?

1. The Zen Peacemakers is an organization dedicated to socially engaged Buddhism. It is within the White Plum Asanga lineage of Taizan Maezumi and was founded in 1996 by Roshi Bernie Glassman and Sandra Jishu Holmes.

Chapter 2: Giving and Receiving

1. Mu Soeng, *Trust in Mind: The Rebellion of Chinese Zen* (Somerville, MA: Wisdom Books, 2015), 14.
2. Thomas Cleary, trans., *Flower Ornament Scripture: A Translation of the Avatamsaka Sutra* (Boston: Shambhala, 1993), 455.

3. Diane Ackerman, *A Slender Thread: Rediscovering Hope at the Heart of Crises* (New York: Vintage Books, 1998), 9.

Chapter 3: Taking Skillful Action

1. Note: Much of the material in chapter 3, "Taking Skillful Action," is adapted from the author's previous book *Waking Up to What You Do* (Boston: Shambhala, 2006).
2. The Three Treasures—Buddha, Dharma, and Sangha— are what sustain us in our path of awakening. Taking refuge in the Buddha is following the path of all those who courageously and sincerely set forth on the path of realizing that there is more to life than what seems familiar and secure. After witnessing old age, sickness, and death in the world around him, Shakyamuni Buddha left the comfort and safety of his home to understand the cause of suffering. Taking refuge in the Dharma is to turn toward the vast ocean of teachings of the Buddha for guidance. Taking refuge in the Sangha brings us together with fellow travelers of the way.

Chapter 4: Practicing Patience

1. Thich Nhat Hanh, *The Heart of the Buddha's Teaching: Transforming Suffering into Peace, Joy, and Liberation* (New York: Broadway Books, 1999), 198.
2. Václav Havel, *The Art of the Impossible: Politics as Morality in Practice* (New York: Fromm International, 1998), 103–14.

Chapter 5: Engaging Effort

1. Dainin Katagiri, *Each Moment Is the Universe* (Boston: Shambhala, 2007), 210.
2. Bodhicitta can be described as the effort to awaken wisdom and compassion for the benefit of all beings.

Chapter 7: Seeing Clearly

1. Charlotte Joko Beck, *Nothing Special* (Boston: Shambhala, 1993), 3.
2. Carlo Rovelli, "All Reality Is Interaction," March 16, 2017, in *On Being,* podcast, https://onbeing.org /programs/carlo-rovelli-all-reality-is-interaction-mar2017/.
3. Stephen Batchelor, *Buddhism without Beliefs: A Contemporary Guide to Awakening* (New York: Riverhead Books, 1997), 82.